MW00626116

Cultural Kaiseki

A Journey Through Offbeat Japan

PHIL LEE

Library of Congress Control Number:
2021904948

ISBN: 978-1-7369976-0-4
Cover design by Simon Thompson
Cover photo by Hassan Pasha on Unsplash
All photos by Phil Lee unless noted

These are my memories, from my
perspective, and I have tried to represent
events as faithfully as possible.

CONTENTS

ACKNOWLEDGMENTS

As with any difficult endeavor, it takes a team of dedicated people to accomplish it well. I could not have done this without the help of many people, but in particular:

- Matt Abiva for being the first person to brainstorm ideas with me and to cheer me along from the beginning.
- Toru Yuhara for helping me with research and to obtain permissions from most of the featured places. He was a huge help!
- Keiko Aoki and Nana Shirakami for helping me with the Japanese language.
- Ken Neville, Badier Velji, Yohei Yamamuro, Rick White, Eric Chumbley, Loretta Peng, and Carol Choy for reading an early draft and providing extensive feedback.
- Karin Taira for supplying additional information and photos from Fukushima.
- My editor Jon Arlan for his professional expertise.
- And to my wife, Carol, and kids, Andrew and Kristen, for letting me go on these trips to begin with, and for putting up with me during months of lockdown due to COVID-19. May we never go through that again!

INTRODUCTION TO KAISEKI (懐石)

It seemed like only a few minutes had passed since I'd sat down at the table and ordered a drink. I hadn't ordered any food yet, but there it was—a small bowl of...something—being placed in front of me by the waitress. She told me what it was in Japanese, which was not very useful for a Korean-born, American-raised, engineering nerd like me.

The food looked visually stunning and equally mysterious, and I was reluctant to disturb this colorful arrangement in front of me. The bowl contained a featureless white cube surrounded by a splash of orange jelly and topped with a sprinkling of red, green, and yellow. I almost thought that dessert had come first, but the aroma gave it away as being something savory. When I went to take a bite, a hint of sesame hit my nose as my palate absorbed an interesting array of spices: a little wasabi, red pepper, vinegar, and citrus. A strange combination for sure, but it all blended in my mouth and came together unlike anything I had tasted before. The flavors were complex but perfectly balanced, with no particular one overpowering the others. Surprised and intrigued, I was hungry for more. I knew something special had just begun.

For many foreigners, the first introduction to Japan is often through food. As one of the most popular cuisines around the world, Japanese food has become ubiquitous nearly everywhere. We've all seen the restaurants in our neighborhoods and at the local food court selling everything from teriyaki to sushi, from tempura to ramen. But a lesser known, and more refined genre of Japanese cuisine exists, called *kaiseki*. It may not be what most people think of when they think of Japanese food, but it may actually be the most Japanese food of all.

Often referred to as the highest level of Japanese cuisine, *kaiseki* is, in some ways, more about the process than the actual food—though, of course, the food is important. It is a dining experience in which a master chef meticulously prepares and serves several small, seasonal dishes, each complementing the others. Over the course of a *kaiseki*, an exquisite meal takes shape. Think of it as a ten-course meal where you don't know what's coming next. The term *kaiseki* roughly translates to "cuisine for a get-together" and is based on traditional Japanese dishes going back hundreds of years. Modern day *kaiseki* has been elevated to an artform balancing flavors, textures, colors, and shapes to create a dazzling treat not only for the palate but for the eyes as well. Beauty, balance, the seasons, and nature are all key ingredients to Japanese culture, and are, likewise, an integral part of a *kaiseki* experience.

I experienced my first *kaiseki* meal in Osaka when I was still a newcomer to Japan. Still not that familiar with Japanese cuisine, I was a bit nervous as I wasn't able to order something off an English menu, but since I was at a business dinner with Japanese colleagues, I went ahead and put my gastronomic fate in their hands.

I'm sure my colleagues as well as the restaurant staff were trying their best to impress us foreign visitors, and they undeniably succeeded. After that first dish of unknown composition (which was delicious by the way), I was ready for more. What came next was a series of delicately arranged appetizers, followed by fresh sashimi, vegetables, some kind of simmered fish and tofu (I think), grilled fish, an assortment of pickles, grilled eel with rice, soup, and finally dessert, a parfait of the freshest tasting berries I've ever had. The only way I finished it all was due to the fact that each course was small and bite sized. It was the meal of a lifetime. Afterwards, I looked up the restaurant to learn more about what had just happened, and found their motto: "Hospitality that resonates with all five senses." And boy, did it ever.

Each course was perfectly shaped and arranged and color coordinated on a small plate. The waitress, elegantly dressed in a kimono, brought out the dishes and explained the ingredients and preparation. The flavor and texture of each morsel differed from the previous one, but complemented it very nicely. And of course, everything smelled divine. The two-hour experience left my belly stuffed, and my brain in a state of sensory overload. I was physically and mentally exhausted by the end of the meal. All I could do was to sit back, sip some green tea, and think about how the rest of the trip would go.

I was working for Disney at the time designing a new theme park ride that was to be built in Japan. I was visiting the engineers in Japan often to review the designs and oversee the production and testing of a multi-million-dollar ride system. The challenging and exciting work kept me very busy, but I also wanted to spend some free time outside the office. After my *kaiseki* initiation, I looked forward to getting out, seeing the country, and learning more about the culture.

I started my journey into Japanese culture like many

others: as a tourist. I had heard of samurais and ninjas, of sushi and karate, but had no real understanding of the society that produced them. Even now, I don't claim to be an expert on Japan by any means. But I have spent countless weeks in the country—spread over many years—and in that time I have slowly come to appreciate the depth and beauty of the place, the people, and the culture.

Over the years, I have traveled back to Japan many times, working during the week and taking the weekends to venture out as much as possible. This resulted in me going on a series of short—you could say "bite-sized"— outings to wherever seemed interesting and within reach of where I happened to be. After seeing the usual tourist sites, I purposely tried to visit places more and more off the beaten path. It was at those places that I caught glimpses of everyday life and slowly built an image of Japanese culture. Visiting places unseen by most foreigners exposed me to the local life and to aspects of the history and culture previously unknown to me. I found it fascinating and wanted to learn more.

What resulted is a collection of stories and experiences that sum up to an appreciation of what I think makes Japan so unique, beautiful, and rewarding. Although I visited many interesting places, the stories presented here are mere glimpses into the world of Japanese culture. As a foreigner and tourist in Japan, I admit that I may never be able to fully understand three thousand years of Japanese history and culture. Fortunately, culture is a living thing. It exists just as much in the here and now, and can be found, with a little work, in everyday places.

My goal is to encourage the reader to seek out some of Japan's more hidden gems, many of which exist very close to the tourist sites. Not only are they interesting in their own right, but these gems will often offer glimpses into the ideals and concepts that lay the foundations of

Japanese culture. They can give the visitor a better appreciation for the country itself. Whether you are a first-time tourist or a seasoned expat living in Japan, there is always something new to be found just around the corner.

I often think back to that first *kaiseki* meal where, as a newcomer to Japan, I was introduced to a whole new universe of experiences. Life, in many ways, is like a long *kaiseki* experience: a string of short, interrelated events that, layer upon layer, form who we are as individuals. I believe that travel and the experiences that we gather along the way are a great catalyst for learning. It is through my travels in Japan that I have attempted to absorb some of the ideals that I've observed and to make them a part of my own life. This book is a collection of bite-sized stories that will be presented here as a *cultural kaiseki,* a meal of experiences. *Itadakimasu.*[1]

---

[1] *Itadakimasu* is a Japanese phrase said before a meal to convey thanks and appreciation for the food about to be received.

PART I
THE WAY OF ART / GEIDŌ (芸道)

One cannot talk about Japanese culture without touching on the concept of *geidō*. *Geidō* is loosely translated as the belief that the *way* that something is done is just as important as the end result. While the concept originated within the classical arts such as Noh theater, calligraphy, and pottery, a similar level of commitment and dedication to one's task can be seen throughout modern Japan. Whether it's a person designing an airplane, or a sushi chef preparing a meal, or a street sweeper cleaning a neighborhood, the level of pride in workmanship on display in Japan is second to none. After all, it is no accident that Tokyo, the largest metropolitan area in the world, is spotlessly clean. (Well, except for Shinjuku…)

In Japan, masters are regarded as living national treasures, or *Ningen Kokuho*, and it is considered an ultimate achievement for a craftsperson to become a master in his or her field. Individuals and groups are certified as "Preservers of Important Intangible Cultural Properties" or *Jūyō Mukei Bunkazai Hojisha* (重要無形文化財保持者). There is even a government ministry that designates the treasures in several categories including kabuki theater, music, dance, ceramics, woodworking, lacquerware, papermaking, bamboo weaving, metalworking and many others.

Of all the locations I've visited in Japan, several come to mind when thinking of master craftsmen. But two sites that stand out in particular are the Seki Traditional Swordsmith Museum in Gifu, and the Nikko Woodcarving Center in Tochigi. These venues, well off the beaten path, are excellent examples of places that are preserving *geidō* or the "way of art."

Gifu Prefecture
岐阜県

CHAPTER 1
SAMURAI SWORDS / KATANA (刀)
Seki, Gifu Prefecture

I headed out into the Japanese countryside alone. The small town of Seki in Gifu Prefecture is around 130 miles from where I was staying in Osaka, and I knew that getting there would be a bit challenging. Osaka Station to Seki Station took a little over two-and-a-half hours and required taking four different trains. First, a local train to Shin-Osaka where I caught the Shinkansen "bullet train" to Nagoya. Then, two more local trains, one of them being a single car, diesel engine. After getting lost only once, I finally arrived in Seki, far off the beaten path, excited to find what I'd come looking for: swords. Seki, after all, has been producing swords, including the katana (better known as the samurai sword) for over six hundred years. So what better place to find a master?

As a fan of old samurai movies, I'd long been fascinated with swords. Their power, lethality, and indestructability (at least in the movies) were second in my mind only to their beauty and grace. As I learned more about the *katana*, my engineering mind became fascinated with the construction and metallurgy of these masterpieces. The fact that over a thousand years ago people developed such advanced techniques without the knowledge of modern chemistry and metallurgy is quite extraordinary. There were no textbooks on the microstructure of steel and what differentiates pearlite from martensite. Nor were there any formulas dictating the carbon content ideal for strong materials. There was only charcoal, iron sand, clay, water, and lots and lots of trial and error. If that's not dedication to a craft, then I don't know what is.

I found my swords at the Seki Traditional Swordsmith Museum (関鍛冶伝承館), a living, working facility that produces handmade swords. There, I attended a live demonstration that showed how the swords are made in the traditional manner. A working metal shop was setup just outside the museum, and was fully outfitted with a furnace and metal working tools. An announcer explained every step of the process as it was demonstrated to the gathered crowd. While there was definitely a lack of English, from what I already knew about swordsmithing and with my limited Japanese, I was able to get the gist of everything and could see the processes that I had read about come to life.

The traditional steel used in Japanese sword making is known as *tamahagane* (玉鋼) or "jewel steel." It is made in a charcoal-fired furnace called a *tatara*, which smelts the iron-rich sand called *satetsu,* usually imported from Shimane Prefecture. The highlight of my visit was when the glowing *tamahagane* was removed from the furnace for the waiting swordsmiths. The master swordsmith held the red-hot metal on an anvil, while two others started rhythmically beating it with their sledgehammers. Intense concentration and coordination were required to hit the small piece of metal accurately, but also to not hit their fellow swordsmiths.

The smell of burnt charcoal was everywhere as sparks

flew out after each hammer blow. THUD! THUD! The sound of the pounding sledgehammers drowned out the noise from the crowd, even as the excitement grew. Safety barriers were in place for the assembled crowd, but I was still close enough to feel the heat coming from the furnace.

Once the metal was pounded flat, the master swordsmith folded the piece to make a thicker block so that the process could start all over again. Normally taking weeks, this tedious work results in a piece of steel pure enough to go on to the subsequent process of quenching. The quenching process is where the magic happens. Without the aid of modern metallurgy or YouTube, the ancient craftsmen figured out that when red-hot steel is quenched in liquid, it becomes much stronger. In fact, the speed at which the steel cooled made a big difference in how hard or brittle it became. The harder the steel, the sharper it can be made. But if it's too hard, it becomes brittle and could break during battle. By applying different amounts of clay to the steel to control the rate of cooling, a sword can be made hard and sharp on the cutting side, and flexible and strong at its core and spine. This differential hardening also gives the sword its sexy curve. Since the blade and the spine cool and contract at different rates, it bends the sword into its final, characteristic shape. Just think of all the years of trial and error, and all the backbreaking work that had to be done to discover and perfect such fine techniques. Standing there that day and watching it happen, it boggled my mind.

Having a museum to preserve the ancient arts and culture is one thing. But why continue to produce swords in the old traditional way? Contrary to popular belief, the steel used in historical Japanese swords is not indestructible. In fact, it is not even that good compared to modern steel. *Tamahagane* is usually so full of impurities that the swordsmith had to pound the steel over and over to bring the impurities to the surface and out of the core metal. Modern steel mills can certainly match, if not better the quality and strength of *tamahagane*. But that would not be true to the concept of *geidō*, where the end result is only a small part of the achievement. The traditional process to get there is just as important and is, for the masters as well as myself, what makes the objective extraordinary.

The same can be said of travel in Japan and this journey in particular. In a strange way, the complicated, four-train path I took to get to Seki made the experience that much more enjoyable. Heading out on my own with a sense of adventure, I could really appreciate the idea of *geidō* in a different way. Even though traveling within Japan is relatively easy for non-Japanese speaking tourists, venturing out off the beaten path to discover new aspects of Japanese culture is a rewarding experience and the trip to Seki remains a cherished memory.

Sidenote on traveling in Japan:
Japan is about the size of California, so traveling from one end to the other (excluding the remote islands) is not difficult even for foreigners. At the time of writing this book, I have been to more than forty countries on six continents, and I can safely say that the public transportation in Japan is by far the best in the world. It is clean, safe, reliable and punctual, usually to a few seconds. The fact that it is so heavily train-based makes it all the better. I LOVE trains and navigating the Japanese countryside on trains is among my favorite travel experiences. With a good train scheduling app and Google Maps, you can go just about anywhere.

Photos taken at the traditional sword forging
demonstration (古式日本刀鍛錬の実演にて撮影)

Hammering the red-hot *tamahagane*

Polishing and sharpening the swords by hand

Sharpening the blade

The *Hamon* (刃文) literally meaning "blade pattern" is the result of the clay that is applied to the blade during the quenching process. Swordsmiths through the centuries developed their own styles and patterns of *Hamon*.

Museum pieces on display

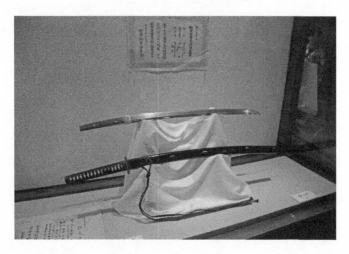

Seki is also the modern kitchen cutlery center of Japan, and during the weekend of my visit was the annual *Hamono Matsuri* (刃物まつり) or Cutlery Festival.

Tochigi Prefecture
栃木県

CHAPTER 2
WOODCARVING IN NIKKO
KIBORI (木彫り)
Nikko, Tochigi Prefecture

At the end of a long week in a conference room near Tokyo reviewing the detailed engineering design of a new ride system in development, my colleagues and I thought it was time for a change in setting. It was autumn and we wanted to get outside to enjoy the cool fresh air and to go sightseeing. After some research, we decided to go to Nikko.

Nikko is a popular tourist destination for Tokyoites and foreigners alike. At only two hours away from Tokyo by train, it makes for a great day trip to see beautiful autumn colors, waterfalls, hiking trails, and historic temples. The shrines and temples of Nikko, a UNESCO World Heritage Site, are known for the intricately carved wooden structures and facades.

One of the main sites, *Tōshōgū Shrine* (東照宮), is a lavishly decorated shrine consisting of more than a dozen structures in the middle of a forest. Beautiful woodcarvings and gold leaf are used abundantly to decorate the buildings in a style not often seen in Japan, where minimalist designs are far more common. One of the woodcarvings depicts three wise monkeys, or the *San Zaru* (三ざる): *Mizaru* (見ざる), *Kikazaru* (聞かざる), and *Iwazaru* (言わざる), or "see not, hear not, and speak not." While the concept is likely to have originated from the "Analects of Confucius" from China, this four-hundred-year-old woodcarving is the original and oldest surviving depiction of the notion popularized as "see no evil, hear no evil, and speak no evil."

As crowded as these sites can get, there are still places nearby that get almost no tourists at all. About a thirty-minute walk from the UNESCO World Heritage site is the Nikko Woodcarving Center (日光木彫りの里工芸センター). Away from all the tourists, this place carries on the art of woodcarving using only traditional hand tools. Sounding sufficiently exotic and very much like a unique experience, my friends and I added it to the list of things to do that weekend. After seeing the major sites, we navigated away from the beaten path. With no English signs to guide us, we walked into the nearby town and made our way to the small unassuming building which housed the Nikko Woodcarving Center.

When we first entered, we had no idea of what to do. The place was so empty, it almost seemed closed. But we did see an older lady sitting behind a counter with some wood pieces, which gave us hope.

When traveling alone in Japan, I am constantly mistaken for a Japanese person. As a person of Korean descent, I suppose I am, genetically, as close to Japanese as you can get without actually being Japanese. (One time, an old lady sitting next to me on a train told me that my face looked very Japanese. At least that's what I *think* she said about my face.) Luckily, this time around I had two friends with me, Eddy and Rick, who are very non-Japanese looking, so it was obvious that we needed some special assistance. After some broken Japanese and a lot of pointing and pantomiming, we were given blank pieces of wood and shown to the classroom.

In the classroom stood a man who looked to be in his seventies and who had probably been carving wood most his life. He quickly ushered us in, gave us some tools, and started to lecture us on how to carve our wood pieces. Unfortunately, the course was all in Japanese, and very fast Japanese at that. We had no hope of following along. (I did manage to catch the phrase *"hidarikiki,"* meaning left-handed, and guessed we were being asked if we need special tools.) The cutting tool was a simple metal blade, formed into a V-shaped hook with a wooden handle. Probably designed four hundred years ago, they had clearly been perfected for the task at hand.

Undaunted, albeit a bit confused, we all started to carve away. The actual carving wasn't difficult, as I'm sure we got the absolute beginner's course. We just had to follow a pre-painted pattern to carve off the varnish. I chose a round plate of about eight inches in diameter and carved an image of bamboo trees. Holding the tool with a fist as you would an ice pick, I slowly carved about one to two millimeters deep into the surface with short pulling motions. I had to be careful not to cut too deep, or the V-shaped blade would cut too wide of a line or even get stuck in the wood. Cut too shallow, and the lines would be too thin and look like mere scratches. It was a delicate balance to get the right depth and width, to make the carving look organic but not too chaotic. We made good progress, but we were taking longer than expected. The instructor waited patiently, looking over our work from time to time. I could tell that he wanted to give us advice but couldn't overcome the language barrier. Unfortunately, we stayed past their closing time and eventually we were the only ones left. Still, the instructor kindly waited for us to finish and once we had, he cleaned each piece for us to take home.

Even though our experience was basic at best, I could tell that this facility did their utmost to preserve the traditional art of the region. And it is in these places where culture lives and thrives. Sure, we could have carved some wooden plates anywhere, but to do it in a place where the tradition goes back four hundred years gave us a better appreciation of the rich history of the area and the art of woodcarving.

The display case in the lobby

An empty classroom

The instructor looks on

The finished carving

The Nikko Woodcarving Center and the Seki Traditional Swordsmith Museum are great examples of organizations that are preserving *geidō* or the "way of art." Some other places worth visiting are:

- Kyoto Samurai Experience – for a chance to wield a *katana*.

- National Bunraku Theater in Osaka – to watch a Tea Ceremony in person and performances with puppets similar to *kabuki* theater.

- Takasawa soba making shop in Nagano – to make your own soba noodles.

- Mochi pounding at Nakatanidou in Nara – to watch how *mochi* (rice cakes) are made.

- Suntory Yamazaki Distillery in Osaka – to see how Japan's oldest distillery makes some of the finest whiskey in the world.

These places also practice their respective art forms and offer wonderful glimpses into Japanese culture.

PART II
TRADITION / DENTŌ (伝統)

In the West, tradition gets a bad rap. American culture is all about progress and forward movement. We're often told that "those who cannot remember the past are condemned to repeat it."[2] Well, this implies a past that was full of mistakes. But what about a past rich with culture? Then it's not a problem to repeat it. Sure, not everything is worthwhile, but a respect for history, for one's ancestors, the elderly, and traditional customs are quintessential aspects of Japanese culture.

Not that Japan doesn't look forward. Japan is, at the same time, one of the most technologically advanced societies on earth. But despite Japan's love for modern technology, the culture retains a deep emphasis on tradition.

Nowhere is this sense of the past on better display than at traditional festivals, or *matsuri*. They happen practically every month all over the country, celebrating

---

[2] George Santayana (1905) *The Life of Reason*

the local history and culture. Some festivals, such as the Snow Festival in Sapporo, the Nebuta Festival in Aomori, the Gion Festival in Kyoto, and the Kanda Festival in Tokyo, attract millions of people, and have become some of the largest events in Japan. Good luck finding some peace and quiet at those locations! Fortunately, there are many other places with festivals of their own that showcase slices of Japanese culture on a slightly smaller scale.

Niigata Prefecture
新潟県

CHAPTER 3
KITE BATTLE / *IKA GASSEN* (いか合戦)
Sanjo, Niigata Prefecture

I landed at Niigata airport, on the central west coast of Japan, and immediately saw proud displays of their local culture. There were shops selling gift packets of their famously delicious rice, along with hundreds of bottles of locally produced *saké*.[3] Then I saw a huge display of kites and a sign in English reading, "Giant Kite Battle Festival." The kites on the display in the airport looked to be real kites and were at least ten feet tall. Wow, I thought. I had never heard of such a festival and was intrigued right away. Unfortunately, the timing wasn't right on that particular trip, but I made a mental note to return someday to see it for myself.

That day came one summer a couple years later, when I returned to Niigata with my friend and co-worker Mike. Together, we were headed to the Sanjo Kite Festival known locally as *Ika Gassen* or kite battle.

---

[3] The Japanese word *saké* means alcohol in general. What Americans call *saké* is actually called *nihonshu* (日本酒) meaning Japanese wine.

Sidenote on kites:
Kites were called *ika-nobori,* or flying squid, in the early 1600s but later came to be called *tako* or octopus, especially near Tokyo. The word *tako* if written in kanji (Chinese characters) like 凧 means kite. This kanji actually originated in Japan and is said to represent "cloth filled with wind." Kites are still called *ika* and *ika-nobori* in some parts of Japan including Niigata.[4] This is why the event is called *Ika Gassen* and not *Tako Gassen.*

The small town of Sanjo is one train-stop south of Niigata and gets very little visitation by foreigners. I had stayed in Sanjo a few times for business, so was somewhat familiar with the area. But the location of this festival was not near a train station. So, I printed out the name of the festival and the rough location and hoped a taxi driver would know where to go. It was only a mile away, so Mike and I could walk there if we had to. When the time came, we found a taxi driver, showed him the location, and he nodded and took off. A few minutes later he pulled over in the middle of a long stretch of road and pointed to a nearby hill. I didn't see anything up there, but he was clearly telling us to go that way. Google Maps agreed, so we got out and started walking.

As we crested the hill, I saw a huge open area larger than a football field. A hundred people dressed in colorful traditional clothing were busily working on preparing their giant kites. They seemed to be organized into teams (called *kumi*) and were getting ready to battle. It was a beautifully sunny day with clear blue skies; a perfect setting for kite flying.

Before the battle could begin, several speeches and formalities had to be conducted, which seemed to drag on for hours. I had no idea what they were saying,

---

[4] Ogawa Naoyuki, "Kites, Bringers of Good Luck," Kokugakuin University Dept. of Japanese Literature and Cultural Traditionology.

but they appeared to be local politicians and officials. Finally, the long procession of officials came to an end, and the festival kicked off with a performance by a highly energetic group of Taiko drummers. With Sado Island and its Taiko Center (*Tatakokan*) just off the coast of Niigata, the tradition of Taiko drumming is strong in this area. In fact, one of the most famous Taiko groups, *Kodō* (鼓童), is based on Sado Island. (The Sado Island Taiko Center also holds events and drumming lessons for the general public, so that's an experience definitely on my to-do list.)

As our attention turned back to the main event, each *kumi* started their flight preparations. The kites were hexagonal in shape and approximately eight to ten feet tall. One of them looked to be over fifteen feet tall. They were traditional in construction, made from wooden rods and paper skins. Every kite was ornately decorated and hand painted with traditional images of famous samurai warriors. Attached to each kite was a sturdy rope, but, curiously, no tails that I could see. I later found out that these particular kites were called Rokkaku (六角) which means hexagonal. They are known for their ease of construction and stable flight characteristics. Invented in Sanjo, they're sometimes called Sanjo-Rokkaku.

As the kites took off, teams of five to ten people would run down the field with the rope in tow. As a kite gained altitude, the people running would let go of the rope one-by-one, so that the kite could go higher and higher. This continued until the last man running ran out of space and held the kite steady in his hands. The actual kite flying was less about combat, and more about controlling the kites in the air, which was disappointing to me at first. But watching dozens of giant kites take to the air was impressive, nonetheless.

The kites were incredibly stable in the air. I was impressed at how such a large and heavy object made of wood and paper could stay aloft for so long. It wasn't a particularly windy day either. As the teams got used to flying their kites, some of them did seem to interact with each other, although it was difficult for me to understand the strategy behind their moves. Some kites were more active in the air as their teams below ran around, while others seemed content to just fly steadily on. A few kites did come crashing down, to the dismay of their handlers, but it wasn't quite the *Battle Royale* that I had hoped for. Still, despite the lack of violent clashes, everyone seemed to be having a great time. There were kids running alongside their parents as they launched the kites. Plenty of people were falling down, either tripping over themselves while running, or from sheer exhaustion. Laughter and cheers filled the air. It was easy to imagine this very *matsuri* happening four hundred years ago, when the first Sanjo Kite Festival took place. Back then, in 1649, the children of local government officials battled the village children with their homemade kites. Ever since, the festival has become a major event between neighboring towns.

After several rounds of "battle," Mike and I noticed that we had lost track of time somewhat and had to get back to the train station. By this point, taxis were nowhere to be seen, so we decided to walk back to the station. Unfortunately, we were getting really behind schedule and had to start running. After the worst mile run in history, we made it back to Tsubame-sanjo Station where Mike barely caught the train back to Niigata Station and the airport to fly home. We parted ways at the station, as I was heading back to Tokyo for additional meetings. But since I had another day to kill over the weekend, I decided to stay in the area a little longer.

In fact, I had plans to go see something that until recently I never knew existed in Japan: bull fighting.

A Taiko drum performance kicks off the festival.

The *kumi* (kite teams) assemble.

The *kumi* display their kites.

A *Sanjo-Rokkaku* Kite

The kites take to the air.

The battle begins.

CHAPTER 4
BULL FIGHTING / TŌGYŪ (闘牛)
Ojiya, Niigata Prefecture

I thought that I was already off the beaten path at Sanjo, but my next destination made that small town look like a metropolis. About an hour south is an even smaller town called Ojiya. Even though the Shinkansen tracks pass nearby, no high-speed trains stop at Ojiya. To get there, you have to take a much slower and smaller train.

Once I arrived in Ojiya, I had planned to leave my luggage in a locker so that I could travel to the bull fighting arena a few miles away. But of course, Ojiya is not Tokyo, and there were no lockers to be found at such a small train station. Miraculously, however, there was a taxi waiting curbside. Probably one of only a few taxis in this entire area, I thought. But maybe with the bull fight, there was a crowd in town? Counting my blessings, I got in the cab and showed him on my phone where to go. He knew right away, so it's safe to say that the arena was the main attraction in town. At least that day.

The arena was about as small as I expected, but more crowded. Again, there were no lockers in sight. I dragged my bag through the dirt to the entrance, bought a ticket, and entered the facility. At the center was the fighting ring—a rectangular dirt field about the size of a baseball diamond, wetted down to be almost muddy. Railings surrounded the perimeter with bleacher type seating all around. A roof structure provided shade to some of the seats, but those seats were more expensive. So I ended up in the open air: the cheap seats. It was a beautifully sunny day. And though the smell of cow manure was in the air, it wasn't as strong as on a typical farm. The slight breeze helped, too.

The field was empty when all of a sudden, a huge bull with horns each more than a foot long came charging in. I didn't see it at first, but the bull had reins that were held by a guy running alongside. They were quickly followed by five more guys, all dressed in traditional robe-like vests (called *happi*) adorned with their team colors and symbols. I was a bit confused. "Are six guys going to fight the bull?" I wondered. I was trying to figure out the rules, when a second bull with a second team of guys entered the arena. It became clear that this was a team battle, and that bull fighting meant that two bulls would fight each other, and not a matador as in Spain. It also became evident that this was more like a Sumo match, in which the wrestlers tried to best the opponent with strength and balance, rather than violence. No blood would be spilt today.

After trotting around the arena a bit, the bulls eventually butted heads and locked horns. The people in the ring backed off and shouted encouragements to their respective animals. The bulls dug in, pushed forward, side stepped, and wrestled each other to what seemed to me like a stalemate. At times when the action seemed to be too slow, guys in the ring gently slapped the backs of the bulls in encouragement to get them to fight harder. The bulls would push and push and push until the one of them backtracked and was forced to disengage. If one bull got the upper hand and pushed the other one down to the ground, the people jumped in and pulled the aggressive bull back so that no animal got hurt. But for the most part, each pair seemed to be evenly matched with the bulls pushing each other back and forth in the arena.

I watched, amazed at how powerful yet gentle these giants could be. I would have been afraid to be in the same ring as these animals, but the bulls seemed to know what to do—and what not to do. They never made any aggressive moves toward the men in the ring. At one point, a small boy even entered the ring with a bull in tow. I guess the bulls were well trained!

Not surprisingly, as I was way off the normal tourist track, the crowd was all locals. I spotted no tourists whatsoever. I was the lone outsider, obvious with my luggage and bright yellow, North Face backpack. I sat next to an elderly couple who probably came here often. The older man cheered the bulls on now and then and kept saying things to his wife. It took me a while to notice that he was actually speaking to me as well! This came as a surprise, since strangers in Japan, particularly in big cities, do not often talk to each other, let alone foreigners. I was definitely not in Tokyo anymore. I've actually found that people in the countryside are much more open and friendly, even to a *gaijin* (foreigner).

As soon as I told the old man that I was American, his face lit up and he tried to speak as much English as he knew. His English was about as bad as my Japanese, but it was enough. We got along fabulously! I told him where I was from, and that I was on a business trip and heading to Tokyo later that day. He seemed genuinely excited to meet a foreigner and said a lot of things in English that made absolutely no sense to me. I'm sure he thought the same of my Japanese!

As the afternoon wore on, several more pairs of bulls came and went. All the matches seemed to end in a draw, at least to my untrained eyes. I needed to get back to Tokyo that evening, so not wanting to repeat the run to the train station earlier that day, I asked the old man if there were any taxis nearby. His expression answered "no," but he got up and gestured for me to stay while he walked away. He made his way to the ticket desk, where I could see him talking to one of the ladies there. After some bowing to the ladies, he returned and told me in Japanese that a taxi would be here in twenty minutes. Great! I thanked him and we continued to enjoy the festivities for a few more minutes.

I was genuinely sad to leave and head back to the big city. These outings into the rural countryside were a refreshing change of pace from the hectic city life, and a great way to see age-old traditions come to life. I vowed then and there to see more of the country.

The arena

Bull fighting / Tōgyū (闘牛)

Locked horns

The bulls are tame when not fighting.

Kyoto
京都府

CHAPTER 5
TEA FARM / CHABATAKE (茶畑)
Wazuka, Kyoto Prefecture

The hillside before me was covered with rows and rows of neatly trimmed, green bushes. "This," said the guide, "is where tea comes from."

Cha (or tea) is my drink of choice. Particularly Japanese tea, which I find smooth and not too bitter. For a while, I had wanted to learn more about how it was made and where it came from. So, when I got the chance, I visited a tea farm located close to Nara, where I happened to be working at the time. It was the perfect opportunity to learn about tea and its ancient roots in Japanese culture. Tea first arrived in Japan when Buddhist monks brought seeds from China in the eighth century. In 1191, a Zen Buddhist monk named Myōan Eisai (明菴 栄西) introduced tea plants to various parts of Japan including Kyoto, then the imperial capital of Japan. In 1211, Eisai wrote one of the first books ever on tea in Japan titled, *Kissa Yojoki* (喫茶養生記), which means "Drink Tea and Prolong Life." In it he described the medicinal nature of tea, and how to grow and process the tea leaves. Eisai also introduced tea to the samurai class and is generally credited with popularizing tea in Japan.

One of the areas that first started large scale tea cultivation was Uji, a city just south of Kyoto. Filling the demand for tea from the imperial capital and beyond, Uji and the nearby Wazuka became the prime producers of *honcha* (本茶) or "real tea," as opposed to the tea from other areas, (sorry, Lipton).

Today, tea production is a multibillion-dollar industry complete with huge farms and processing plants. However, the tradition of small farms is still alive and well and it is not that difficult to find one if you know where to look. My tea education started in Wazuka, one of the aforementioned areas of tea history. About eight centuries ago, while Genghis Khan was conquering most of Eurasia, and the Pope was sending Crusaders into the Middle East, locals began growing tea in Wazuka. Even today, Wazuka is a tiny town of less than four thousand people, many of whom come from tea farming families. While Shizuoka and Kagoshima lead the way in tea production volume, Wazuka and Uji are well known for their high-quality green teas.

One of the farmers in Wazuka is Tanaka Daiki, founder of d:matcha. Born and raised in Tokyo and educated in Kyoto and Boston, he lived and worked in cities until deciding to create a different kind of business in the countryside. He wanted to improve society by producing and promoting tea and other healthy foods in Japan. The d:matcha website lists three major goals as their vision:

1. Sustaining the culture of Japanese tea farming and the environment,
2. Producing health from farm to table,
3. Passing the passion for this culture on to a local and global audience.

When I came across their website, I was intrigued and wanted to learn more about tea farming. I saw that they offered tours of their farm and a behind-the-scenes look at tea processing, so immediately signed up. The train ride from Nara only took fifteen minutes, and I met up with Daiki-san at Kamo Station. A quick car ride later, we arrived at the main d:matcha store in Wazuka.

After dropping off my bags at the store, we got in the car again to drive up the nearby hills where the tea fields were located. We first visited a shrine on a local mountain and hiked up a hundred steps. It was a peaceful setting, which allowed us to gaze upon the tea fields all around.

We then walked into the tea fields to get a closer look. Daiki-san provided plastic bags, which were to be filled with tea leaves of my picking. As I strolled through the rows of tea plants, I looked for perfectly shaped leaves that were one to two inches long, which Daiki-san said tasted the best. I hand-picked about a dozen such medium-sized leaves, which ended up being part of my lunch later that day as a surprise treat.

Tea fields

I learned that tea, including green, oolong, and black tea all came from the same plant, the *Camellia Sinensis*. The difference is in how the tea leaves are processed.

Camellia Sinensis

Green tea is steamed and dried immediately upon harvest. This stops the oxidation process, and results in the most antioxidants in the tea. Oolong tea is the traditional Chinese tea and is made by partially oxidizing the leaves prior to refinement. The black teas of Europe and India are fully oxidized for the strongest flavor and most caffeine.

Green tea leaves can be roasted (to make *hōjicha*) or processed in different ways to produce matcha, sencha, and gyokuro.

Matcha is made by drying and powdering tea leaves and is the highest grade and most famous tea of Japan. From bottled drinks to ice cream flavors to KitKat chocolates, matcha is everywhere in Japan. It was first produced in Uji in the sixteenth century and became an essential part of the tea ceremony, or *chanoyu* (茶の湯).

Sidenote on the tea ceremony:
Nothing is as traditional as the tea ceremony in Japan. Having watched real tea ceremonies a couple of times, I came to the realization that I do not have that kind of patience required for a proper cup of matcha. However, if you are interested in learning more, I would recommend the 2018 film, *Nichinichi Kore Kôjitsu*, or "Every Day a Good Day," which revolves around two young girls learning about the tea ceremony from a master teacher. The teacher was portrayed by the famous actress Kiki Kirin (樹木 希林), who passed away shortly after filming the movie.

Sencha is made by drying and rolling the tea leaves and *not* grinding them into powder. It was invented in 1738 by tea farmer Sōen Nagatani (宗円永谷) a native of Ujitawara, located in-between Uji City and Wazuka. Sōen was a smart businessman as well as a farmer. He knew that conservative Kyoto would not be interested in anything new, so he headed to Edo, which was then the cultural capital of Japan (and soon to become the actual capital, Tokyo).

After a long series of rejections, Sōen brought his new sencha tea to Yamamoto Kahei (山本嘉兵衛), who ran a shop called Yamamotoya (山本屋). Yamamoto was impressed with the new flavor and began selling it under the name *tenka ichi* (天下一) or "first under the heavens." It became a huge hit and Yamamotoyama is still around today. I just had a cup myself.

The final type is called gyokuro and is really another type of sencha—the most expensive kind. Gyokuro is made from tea plants that are grown under a shade for longer periods than regular sencha. The shade limits the sun's breakdown of the chemical theanine, which is the source of sweetness and umami (flavor) in tea. The process of growing plants under a shade is, as you might imagine, a complex process developed through years of trial and error. A famous gyokuro tea is Yamecha, produced in Yame City in Fukuoka Prefecture. (Tip: If you ever fly business class on ANA, then definitely try the Yamecha—and the ramen.)

There are three harvests of tea plants during the year. The first harvest, or "first flush" as it is called, happens in April or May and results in the highest quality tea leaves. These leaves are destined for high-end matcha and sencha products. Tea ceremonies all over Japan will use this premium matcha. The second flush is in July, and these teas typically have a slightly more bitter taste. They are often used to make desserts and lattes. The third flush happens in October and produces the lowest quality tea leaves, which are used for mass-produced bottled drinks. Once harvested, the tea leaves are brought to a small local processing plant, where the farmers can prepare their products for market. Our next stop was at one of these processing plants.

The term "plant" is misleading. The facility we visited was not a large factory, but instead, a small shack out in the countryside. We walked into the wooden building and saw around eight different machines, each with its own function: drying, rolling, cutting, grinding, and so on. Daiki-san explained how the tea leaves would be processed from machine to machine. A farmer would still have to manually operate each machine, but the facility allows small farms to prepare large batches of tea for market. The plant was not in use during our visit so it was quiet and peaceful, but I could imagine how loud and chaotic it might be during full production. It was interesting to see the entire life cycle of tea production, from farm to retail store.

A typical processing facility shared by local farmers

Inside the facility are several manually operated machines for the farmers to process their crops.

Daiki-san explains the process.

This machine rolls the tea leaves.

A traditional stone mill used to grind tea leaves by hand

Tea powder is whisked using a
traditional bamboo *chasen*.

At the end of the tour, I got to make my own matcha and to sample various sencha teas from the farm. The aromas and flavors varied wildly from the usual bitter tea to some that were sweeter and smoother than any tea I'd had before. One particular tea was so strong with umami that I would not have even thought of it as a tea if I weren't at a tea farm. I learned that the temperature of the water also made a difference in how strong the flavor was, and that hotter water should be used on tea leaves that were already used to brew a batch.

The tour ended with some sweet confectioneries baked at the farm using their matcha. As a bonus treat, I got to eat the tea leaves that I had picked earlier. The people at d:matcha used my leaves to make tempura. *Oishii*! (delicious)

Tea leaves tempura style

Matcha flavored sweets

Sampling different types of sencha teas from the farm

Daiki-san and his team at d:matcha are on a mission to revitalize an industry threatened by the migration of younger generations to cities, leaving an aging population and its traditions behind. By educating the general public, including foreigners, a greater appreciation of traditional Japanese tea culture can be promoted to ensure its continuation for years to come.

Much like the traditional vineyards of Europe, the tea farms of Wazuka have been creating a yearly product, based on crops, dependent on weather, and reliant on the skills of the masters over dozens of generations. So, the next time you enjoy a cup of tea, think of all the history and traditions you are holding in the palm of your hand.

People and places preserving the age-old traditions of Japan can be found throughout the land. Some other sites worth visiting are:

- Kyoto's Gion District and Miyako Odori – to see geisha and maiko performances.

- Yasue Gold Leaf Museum in Kanazawa – to see how gold leaf is traditionally made.

- Daiō Wasabi Farm in Nagano – to see how wasabi is grown.

- Nebuta Museum in Aomori – to see the intricate parade floats of the Nebuta Festival.

PART III
THE OLD AND THE NEW

Even with all the emphasis on tradition, modern Japan is a living juxtaposition of its past and its present. It is a place where you find a hundred-year-old shrine next to a twenty-first-century skyscraper, a Buddhist temple in the middle of downtown metropolis. You might see people wearing kimonos to work, using their smartphones to play Pokémon Go while walking past a two-hundred-year-old restaurant in the middle of modern Tokyo.

Take, for instance, the ancient city of Kyoto, *the* place to see temples, shrines, castles, samurai-era homes, tea ceremonies, geisha dance performances, kabuki, and every other feature of traditional Japanese culture. It served as the nation's capital and the cultural epicenter for over a thousand years. Much of that history and culture survives to this day with seventeen UNESCO World Heritage sites in Kyoto and nearby suburbs.

Sidenote on Kyoto:

Kyoto was spared much of the bombing during WWII and was originally a top target for the atomic bomb toward the end of the war. However, U.S. Secretary of War Henry L. Stimson took Kyoto off the list because he deemed it an important cultural center, saying that it "must not be bombed." Stimson knew this of Kyoto because he had been there; he and his wife had traveled to this city on their honeymoon.

Maybe if we all traveled more, there would be fewer places that we'd want to bomb.

With all its history, Kyoto is also the home to a thriving I.T. industry with several hi-tech electronics companies based there. It is also home to Nintendo and one of the Toei movie studios. The Kyoto train station is one of the largest and most modern train stations I have ever seen. A fifteen-story high roof encloses dozens of train lines and platforms, probably a hundred shops and restaurants, and a vast network of underground facilities. Kyoto Station is also located about a thousand feet from Higashi Honganji Temple, originally built in 1604. The temple's main hall is one of the largest wooden structures in the world and doesn't look at all out of place in the middle of this beautiful city.

At peak times, a Tōkaidō Shinkansen bullet train leaves Kyoto Station around every five minutes and carries more than 460,000 passengers daily. This technological marvel is named after and roughly follows the path of the 400-year-old Tōkaidō Road (東海道) from Kyoto to Edo (modern day Tokyo). Throughout Japan, you can find countless examples of the old and new coexisting in physical and cultural harmony. Temples, shrines, and museums—where cultural heritage is preserved within contemporary architecture and modern neighborhoods—are perfect places to explore this idea.

Edo (Tokyo)
江戸 (東京都)

CHAPTER 6
THE 47 RONIN / AKŌ-RŌSHI (赤穂浪士)
Edo

Located in the same Minato Ward as Tokyo Tower and the glitzy Roppongi, Sengakuji (泉岳寺) Temple is rarely visited by foreign tourists. Few Japanese go there, either. Tucked away next to a university, a high school, and some residential apartments, the temple is a modest collection of totally ordinary buildings. What's exceptional about Sengakuji is its infamous past. Three hundred years ago, the temple saw the real-life events of the story of the 47 Ronin, or the "Ako Incident"—a tale of honor, sacrifice, samurai loyalty, and vengeance. Retold a thousand times in books, television, movies, operas, plays, paintings and even in *kabuki*, the story has become legendary in Japan and beyond.

As the popular story goes, a master of ceremonies (an important position back in the day) named Kira Yoshinaka (吉良義央) offended a feudal Lord named Asano Naganori (浅野長矩) so much so that Asano attacked Kira at Edo Castle, a crime punishable by death. As punishment, Asano was forced to commit suicide,

59

leaving his band of samurai without a master, thus becoming *ronin*.

The *ronin* blamed Kira for their master's death and plotted to kill him as revenge, taking almost two years to finally do it. Once accomplished, they presented Kira's decapitated head to their master Asano's grave at Sengakuji and turned themselves in for judgement. The *ronin* were then sentenced to ritual suicide of their own, but they were publicly seen as being honorable and brave for avenging their master.

That's the simple version of the story. The truth is much more complicated with political intrigue, blind loyalties, and contradicting accounts. For instance, there are many accounts of Asano being completely at fault and deserving of his fate. Kira, who is traditionally portrayed as the bad guy, may have just been a decent man going about his business.

Also, when Asano died and left his men to become *ronin*, there were hundreds of them, and not just forty-seven. The others went on with their lives, got jobs, and took care of their families. The forty-seven, on the other hand, devoted themselves to bloody revenge, knowing they would inevitably die as well. Call that courage and loyalty...or something else.

While the actual events of 1701 and 1702 have been somewhat blurred by the myths and dramatic retellings that followed, the places involved have been preserved and can be easily visited today. I visited Sengakuji Temple in the middle of Tokyo on a cold winter morning. After navigating a labyrinth of walkways through the surrounding neighborhood, I finally found the temple; it looked like any other "old" building in Japan. The complex included a temple and a museum dedicated to the 47 Ronin and their story. Within the museum were life-sized statues of each *ronin* with their name, age, and a description of their involvement. The museum was nice, but the main attraction, to me, was the grave site of the 47 Ronin and their fallen leader Asano located in a courtyard just outside the museum.

The graves were neatly arranged in rows with large tombstones bearing their names. The tomb of the master Asano, off to one side, overlooked the forty-seven who were all together, side by side, in a square-shaped landing. Burnt incense sticks lay by the tombs, adding a faint scent to the air. Despite the age of the cemetery, everything was spotlessly clean and immaculately kept. The stonework all looked intact and large wooden handrails (probably a modern addition) finished off the area. As I exited the grave site, I noted a small hole in the ground, cordoned off by a stone handrail. A sign on the railing identified this as the well where the *ronin* washed and prepared the decapitated head of Kira before presenting it to their master's grave. The simple well could easily have been missed. Looking at it, I could imagine the *ronin* crouching down near the well to wash off the bloody head of Kira. The whole story comes to life when you have the chance to stand right where it happened.

Despite the bloody history that made the temple famous, it is now a very nice and peaceful place to visit. A quiet oasis in the middle of an urban jungle, it offers the chance to step back in time into the Edo Period. It is a great reminder that even in the middle of modern-day Tokyo, a three hundred-year-old story can be re-awakened just by taking a short detour to a place not often visited.

Sidenote on the Edo Period:

The period from 1603 to 1868, when the Tokugawa Shogunate (aka *Shogun*) ruled Japan from Edo, is called, appropriately enough, the Edo Period or Edo Jidai (江戸時代). While the symbolic capital as well as the figurehead emperor remained in Kyoto, the *Shogun*, and his *Daimyo,* or regional feudal lords, and the samurai class effectively ruled Japan. The Edo Period was a time of peace, economic growth, and tremendous artistic and intellectual development. *Kabuki* theater was born, and *Sumo* wrestling became a profession. The artist *Hokusai* published his "Thirty-six Views of Mount Fuji" series of woodblock prints, which included "The Great Wave off Kanagawa" destined for modern T-shirts everywhere. The term *geisha* was coined to refer to popular entertainers of music and dance. *Manga* became popular, and the art of *bonsai* plants reached a peak. In fact, the oldest surviving *bonsai* plant was created during the Edo Period and is now kept at the Imperial Palace in Tokyo. And, most important of all (to me personally), *Edomae nigiri sushi* was invented.

Sengakuji

The grave sites

A map of the gravesites

The "head washing" well

Signage explaining the well

首洗い井戸

義士が本懐成就後、吉良上野介の首級をこの井戸水で洗い、主君の墓前に供え報告したところから「首洗い井戸」と呼ばれています。

⑩ Kubi-Arai (head washing) Well

After the retainers accomplished their avenge by killing Kira, they marched to Sengakuji to report to their lord's grave. When they arrived, they first washed Kira's decapitated head (kubi) at this well and then laid it in front of their lord's grave and announced their success.

Nagano Prefecture
長野県

CHAPTER 7
HOKUSAI MUSEUM (北斎美術館)
Obuse, Nagano Prefecture

There are several museums housing the Edo Period art of Japan's most famous artist, *Hokusai Katsushika* (北斎葛飾). Two contrasting ones are the often-visited Hokusai Museum in Sumida Ward, Tokyo and the more off the beaten path Hokusai Museum in Obuse, Nagano. Both have their advantages.

The one in Tokyo is a futuristic looking design of modern architecture. Created by the award-winning architect Sejima Kazuyo (妹島和世), the building is clad in aluminum panels creating a collection of unorthodox shapes and angles. So much so that as you approach the building, it is not obvious as to where the entrance is. It is difficult to tell if you are on the front, rear, or side of the building, since it really doesn't have any of those things. When I visited, after standing around confused for a few moments, I saw people walking up and entering, so I followed along. Inside I found a nice collection of his woodblock prints, some history about the artist and how he lived in Sumida, and a full-scale reproduction of his house—complete with mannequins demonstrating how the prints were made. All in all, it is a nice outing in Tokyo, but I believe an even richer experience can be had by going a bit off the beaten path and visiting the Hokusai Museum in Obuse.

The small town of Obuse is nestled among the mountains of Nagano Prefecture and at around thirty minutes from Nagano City by train, it is not at all difficult to visit—not nearly as difficult as it must have been for the eighty-three-year-old artist himself, who came from Edo by foot multiple times. It was in Obuse that he painted several masterpieces, many of which survive to this day.

Being a woodblock print artist meant that Hokusai could mass produce his art and make it affordable to the general public. It is estimated that five thousand copies of his "Great Wave off Kanagawa" were printed from the original woodblocks. Only a few of those originals survive to this day (one of them sold for $471,000 in 2019). But in Obuse, you can still see actual original paintings, not mass-produced prints, of Hokusai's work.

As I walked around the museum in Obuse, I couldn't help but notice the glass-enclosed rooms that housed large wooden wagons. They were parade floats about fifteen feet long by six feet wide by over ten feet high. At the age of eighty-five, Hokusai spent six months in Obuse painting a dragon and a phoenix for the ceiling of a giant float for the Higashimachi festival. Then, in the following year, he painted two "angry waves" in a style similar to that of his masterpiece, "The Great Wave off Kanagawa." The "male" and "female" waves were painted on the ceiling of a parade float for the Kanmachi festival. These paintings are known for the claw-like features given to the waves as they crest and break over the waters below.

Each float had a main body that could hold about six to ten people with a roof structure over their heads. It is this roof structure that held the Hokusai paintings, which I could see from below. During the festivals, large groups of people would pull the floats down a road and the spectators on the sides would have been able to look up to see the paintings on the underside of the ceilings of the floats. These two priceless floats are now designated as Official Treasures of Nagano Prefecture.

But that's not all. The prolific artist saved his best for last. In 1848, the year before his death, Hokusai painted his largest piece yet, a phoenix for the ceiling of Ganshoin Temple in Obuse. At twenty-one by nineteen feet in size, it is an imposing figure looking down at you from above with its large glaring eye that seems to follow you no matter where you go in the temple. For this reason, the painting is called the "Phoenix Staring in Eight Directions." Directly painted on to twelve wooden panels and installed to the ceiling when completed, the painting has remained in excellent condition with all its brilliant colors and gold leaf shining in full glory.

As I entered the small temple and made my way to the central room, I was immediately struck by the enormous creature staring down at me. Unlike any other depiction of a phoenix that I've seen, Hokusai's creation is a collection of feathers short and long, with brilliant streaks of orange, red, blue, green and brown. Several peacock-like feathers with "eyes" adorned the phoenix, while its main eye at the center stared straight down. It was difficult to tell which end was up as the mass of feathers seems to swirl above me. As I walked around the room, I felt the gaze of the phoenix on me no matter where I stood. It was one of the most impressive pieces of art I've seen in Japan. (Too bad photos were not allowed.) But as beautiful as it was, it also made me a little uncomfortable. No one likes to be stared at, even by a mythological creature, so I soon took my leave.

The mile-long walk from Ganshoin Temple back to

Obuse Station was a beautiful one. Strolling through the Nagano countryside, I passed by several farms, an apple orchard, and a vineyard. I could see rows and rows of vines with grapes hanging down from them. The grapes were not fully grown, but well on their way to a full harvest. I learned later that Nagano had the second most wineries in Japan. A good reason to return!

Sidenote on Nagano:
Nagano Prefecture is, in general, a haven for nature lovers. With the Japanese Alps, including most of the Hida, Kiso, and Akaishi Mountains, it's no wonder that it was able to successfully host the 1998 Winter Olympics. It is home to several national parks, as well as resort lakes. Along with its natural beauty and traditional culture, Nagano is also the home to several factories for companies like Citizen (watches), Sony VAIO, and Seiko Epson, proving again that modern Japan can coexist with its classical past.

I will definitely return to Nagano someday, but my thoughts soon turned to eating. Getting a bit hungry, I searched but could not find any restaurants in the vicinity. I figured I would have to wait until I reached the train station, but lo-and-behold, I soon came across a grocery store. It was not a huge supermarket by any means, but I was delighted to see that they had a large selection of prepared foods ready to eat. An informal *kaiseki* meal presented itself to me. All I had to do was to make my selections to go. I chose my favorite bento staples: vegetable tempura, inari sushi (vinegared rice wrapped in fried tofu), and gyoza (dumplings). One of the women on staff kindly microwaved the food for me and smelling the food made me even hungrier, so I decided to eat right away. I had heard that it is frowned upon and even illegal in some areas of Japan to eat while walking, so I had no choice but to wolf down the food while standing in the parking lot. It was not an elegant *kaiseki* experience, but it was satisfying, nonetheless. All in all, the trip to Obuse and Nagano was one of the most peaceful pleasures I've had in Japan.

The Hokusai Museum in Obuse

The Great Wave off Kanagawa (神奈川沖浪裏)

The Parade Floats

The "Male" and "Female" Waves

Obuse Countryside

The Sumida Hokusai Museum in Tokyo

Shiga Prefecture
滋賀県

CHAPTER 8
MIHO MUSEUM
Shiga Prefecture

It's not often that I am forced to leave the trains behind and take a bus in Japan, but when I do, it is always a bit nerve-wracking. First you have to figure out which bus to take and the time schedule. Then getting the correct ticket can be challenging if the buses do not take pre-paid IC cards like Suica, Pasmo, or Icoca cards. Then you have to figure out when to get off the bus, since they do not stop at train stations with big signs on them. In fact, sometimes they do not stop at all unless someone presses a button to let the driver know.

Having taken the wrong bus on a couple occasions in the past, I was relieved when it was clear enough that I got it right on the hour-long ride to a destination that I'd been wanting to visit for months: the Miho Museum.

Deep in the forest, among the mountains of Shiga Prefecture, the museum is one of the best examples of the harmony between man and nature that Japan has to offer. The balance between the traditional and the modern is proudly on display here. But despite all this, and despite the wonderful art inside, I was there to see one thing: the building itself.

The Miho Museum is housed in an architectural wonder designed by the legendary I.M. Pei. The steel and glass structure is a modern take on traditional Japanese architecture integrated seamlessly into its natural surroundings. Resembling a temple from the Edo Period, the exterior and interior are minimalistic in design yet rich in subtle details. This masterful balance of simplicity and complexity is a key feature of the Japanese aesthetic called *shibui* (渋い). The concept of unobtrusive beauty, especially in nature, has deep roots in Japanese culture and is maintained throughout the design of this museum—a perfect mixture of the old and new.

My experience started as soon as I departed the bus and approached the museum on foot. Cherry trees lined the path to the museum, and even though they were not blooming during my visit, the sense of walking *into* nature was profound. I've read that the approach to the museum was inspired by an ancient Chinese folktale of a fisherman who wandered through the woods to find a hidden village full of joy and beauty on the other side. The museum was thus conceived, with the walkway going through a mountain (via a tunnel) to the other side where a beautiful village meets your eyes. The tunnel itself, clad on the inside with brushed stainless-steel panels, is a work of art. After walking through the tunnel, I emerged onto a short bridge suspended by steel cables reaching down from a perfect parabolic arch. As I walked on the bridge, I was again enveloped by trees. In the distance through the trees, I caught my first glimpse of the Miho Museum.

A paved courtyard with a wide granite staircase led up to the building. I noticed the defining feature of the building, the roof, made of glass and steel, still had the distinct look of a traditional temple. The main doors looked like a circular portal that slid open like magical *shoji* screens as I walked in.

The interior immediately greeted me with warm light bouncing off the beige limestone walls, while a series of floor-to-ceiling, panoramic windows showed off the vast valley below. The high angled ceilings gave a sense of spaciousness even in a relatively small structure, and the translucent roof, by allowing natural light to filter through the glass and metal above, helped to make it feel even more open.

The art pieces inside were an afterthought to me initially, but they complemented the interior nicely and created a natural feeling of flow as I walked through the building. The collection of ancient Asian and Western art and artifacts from the Egyptian to the Chinese to the Roman Empires are impressive for a small private collection. (For more information, I'd recommend the museum website.)

The museum also has temporary exhibitions visiting from time to time, and I was fortunate enough to see an exceptional collection of *bizen* (備前焼) pottery from the Momoyama period (1574 to 1600). Traditional *bizen* ware originated in Okayama Prefecture and is characteristically unfinished looking due to the lack of glazing. The artform almost died out during the Meiji Era of the nineteenth century, but *bizen* is making a bit of a comeback with new up-and-coming artists taking up the practice. These new artists, as well as works by Living National Treasures, were part of the exhibit at the museum.

As I made my way through the museum, time seemed to pass quickly. Soon, the sunset came, and a beautiful glow filled the entire interior with a warm and peaceful feeling. A good way to end any day. As I walked back to the bus stop, I was in nature once again, if only for a short time. But heading back to the city, and inspired by my visit to the museum, I vowed to get back to nature as soon as I could.

The approach to the Miho Museum

Crossing the bridge

The front entrance

The entrance lobby

The grand interior

View of the valley below

Other fascinating places where the old coexists with the new are:

- Dogo Onsen in Ehime – one of Japan's oldest hot springs, and inspiration for the bath house in the movie, *Spirited Away*.

- Any of the Japanese Castles, but especially: Himeji, Hikone, Matsue, Matsumoto, and Inuyama Castles which are National Treasures.

- Horikawa Boat Tour in Shimane – a nice boat tour along the 400-year-old canals around Matsue Castle.

- Kenroku-en in Kanazawa – one of the three most beautiful gardens in Japan.

- Ise Grand Shrine in Mie – one of the holiest and most important Shinto shrines.

PART IV
DISCOVERING YOURSELF IN NATURE / KACHOU FUUGETSU (花鳥風月)

When thinking of Japan, foreigners often picture an urban jungle—the hi-tech hustle and bustle of megacities like Tokyo, Yokohama, Nagoya, and Osaka. But in reality, seventy percent of Japan is composed of forests and mountains. The country is a collection of over 6,800 islands, stretching almost two thousand miles from end to end. The main islands consist of many distinct geographical regions, each with their own climate and biodiversity. When traveling from region to region, differences in everything from local food to weather are not only evident, but celebrated.

A profound respect for and appreciation of nature plays a major role in Japanese society. There is a concept called *Kachou Fuugetsu* (花鳥風月), which refers to the belief that when you experience the beauty of nature, you truly discover yourself. This ancient proverb comes from the Noh theater work *Fūshi Kaden* (風姿花伝) written in the 1400s and is considered to be an important part of Japanese aesthetics.

Of course, people are probably not thinking of such deep philosophies every day, but the appreciation and enjoyment of nature is present, nonetheless. Japan is a wonderful country to experience the great outdoors, with limitless hiking, mountain climbing, skiing, and canyoning opportunities, not to mention bike trails that extend from island to island and many other unique adventures not that far off the beaten path.

Hokkaido
北海道

CHAPTER 9
BREAKING THE ICE: AN AFTERNOON
ON THE SEA OF OKHOTSK (オホーツク海)
Monbetsu, Hokkaido

If Okinawa is the Hawaii of Japan, then Hokkaido would be the Alaska. Hokkaido, the largest and northernmost prefecture in Japan, is known for its vast wilderness. It has the lowest population density of any place in the country. Cool in the summer and covered in powdery snow in the winter, Hokkaido is a nature lover's paradise.

Despite being no further north than Oregon or the South of France, Hokkaido gets cold in the winters—really cold. The prevailing winds from the northwest bring arctic cold temperatures directly from Siberia. In January and February of each year, parts of the Sea of Okhotsk off the north coast of Hokkaido become frozen, stopping all maritime traffic—well, almost all traffic.

While respecting nature, but not giving into it, the people of Hokkaido have ships that can tackle the frozen sea and the drift ice that can fill it. Operating from the northern port city of Monbetsu, the Ice Breaker *Garinko II* sails in the harshest of climates to give people an opportunity to see and experience the power of mother

85

nature.

Getting there was a little challenging, but worthwhile. Leaving my beloved trains behind, I flew to Monbetsu from Tokyo on the only flight offered by any airline. ANA operates a small commuter jet once a day, making the journey north easy and comfortable. Once I arrived at the tiny, single-gate airport, I struggled to find the city bus that would take me to the hotel and ended up chickening out and taking a taxi. More than anything, considering how remote the city was, I was glad it still had amenities such as an airport, taxis, hotels, and restaurants. There was, of course, little to no English anywhere. A few key signs here and there helped, but for the most part, I just had to go with the flow.

Two miles of snowed in roads and terrain covered the distance from the hotel to the harbor. A distance that I decided to hike, as the weather wasn't bad at all— probably in the 40s F (around 5 degrees C). With my drone in my backpack, I headed out into the cold. Using Google Maps on my phone, I navigated to the coast, and then toward the port where the ship was docked. I stopped mid-way to get some beautiful drone footage of a frozen harbor and drift ice and then slowly made my way toward the ship.

My friend Yoko had reserved tickets for me for the next day's sunrise cruise, but I wanted to try to get on that day as well. So, I went to the ticket counter and after some excruciatingly bad Japanese, I got the last available ticket on an afternoon voyage. The ship was roomy for the one hundred or so passengers on board, maybe a little more crowded than I had expected, but still nothing like a Tokyo subway. The ship had two levels. The lower level was completely enclosed while the upper level had a large open viewing deck, which is where I found an open spot next to a railing. As we sailed past the breakwater, the wind picked up, temperatures dropped, and I regretted not bringing a heavier coat and gloves. The ice had not made it all the way to shore in the harbor, so the ship had to cruise for a few minutes before reaching the ice field out at sea.

It was late in the season, so the ice pack was already starting to melt. By the time the ship reached the ice field, instead of a crunch or a thud, there was more of a slushing sound like skiing on a warm spring afternoon. In just a few moments, the ship was surrounded by ice as far as the eye could see, frozen from horizon to horizon and looking more like a snowy landscape rather than a sea.

The ice field was composed of several large floating sheets that were starting to crack all around. The ice had snow buildup on top, which made it look like land, except that there was water visible along the cracks. Stretching out to the horizon, the "land" scape reminded me of the white salt flats of Death Valley in California. Some of the ice pieces looked like giant floating lily pads as they crowded together to cover the water surface. When the ship hit the ice, the large sheets either broke up into the water or were pushed off to the side exposing more of the ocean below. Some of those pieces must have weighed tons, but they were easily pushed aside by the ship.

The impressive ship was based on an experimental vessel for the Alaskan oil industry. The original *Garinko* ship started taking passengers into ice fields in 1987. I was on a newer ship, the *Garinko II,* an upgraded 150-ton vessel. The unique ship features two Archimedes screws at the bow, which can pull the vessel up on to a sheet of ice. When the weight of the ship breaks the ice, the propeller in the back takes over to push the ship along. From the lower deck near the bow, you can watch the screws up close as they pull in and crush the ice.

As the ship continued to make its way through the ice, I finished taking my obligatory photographs and videos[5], and stepped back to take a deep, relaxing breath. The cold air no longer bothered me. I felt the excitement of seeing something completely new, and along with it, a tranquil appreciation of how powerful nature can be. I thought of how fortunate I was to be there. The crowd slowly thinned as people became cold and went down into the lower deck, but I remained on top to soak in every minute of this extraordinary place.

I need to return there someday.

---

[5] Video and drone footage can be seen on my YouTube channel: "Adventures with Phil." Subscribe and search for "The Sea of Okhotsk."

The small port town of Monbetsu

The *Garinko II* ice breaking boat

Entering the ice field

Ice as far as the eye could see

Looking back toward shore
and the mountains of Hokkaido

CHAPTER 10
DOG SLEDDING IN SNOWY HOKKAIDO / INUZORI (犬ぞり)
Shikaoi, Hokkaido

Sixteen dogs can get loud. They were all barking and howling as we made our way out of the farm and on to a snow-covered field. When they passed the chain-link fence, they knew they were about to be let loose. Their excitement grew. The huskies were divided into two sled teams of eight. I boarded one of the sleds and held on tightly with a mixture of anticipation, anxiety, and wonder. *How fast were we going to go? Could I control the dogs? Was it going to be dangerous in any way?* After the trainer completed the pre-launch checks, everything was a go! Three...two...one...and then silence. Just the sound of wind through my hair.

Like thousands of other tourists every year, my friends and I had gone to Sapporo, the capital of Hokkaido, to ski. The skiing is phenomenal there. The area around Sapporo, which hosted the 1972 Winter Olympics, is blessed with deep powder snow at mountain resorts less than an hour away from downtown. With almost two million people, Sapporo is a large city on an otherwise sparsely populated island, and tourists flock there to see the annual Snow Festival in February and to enjoy winter sports. So how did we end up on a sled being pulled by dogs in the middle of nowhere? Well, when you are in a stunning place like Hokkaido, there's bound to be something awesome just around the corner, if you take the time to look. During my research of the area, I discovered Mushing Works, a farm that runs dog sledding tours during the winter.

In central Hokkaido is a small town named Shintoku with a population barely over six thousand. Shintoku is difficult to find on a map, but worth visiting, if only to get away from the crowds. (The soba there is also delicious.) After two hours on a local train, we arrived at Shintoku Station to transfer to a pre-arranged taxi, and head to an even smaller town called Shikaoi, which doesn't even have a train station. From there, we headed to Mushing Works. The owner of Mushing Works, Takita Takeshi (also the lead dog trainer), met us and drove us in his car to the farm. The farm was located in a remote snow-covered field, but then again, everything in this area at this time of year is a remote snow-covered field. As we drove into the farm, I could see a large fenced off area with twenty or so cute little dog houses. Some dogs were leashed to the houses, but others were roaming about freely. We received a vocal welcome from the animals.

We warmed up a bit in a small building on the farm before starting the day's adventure. Takeshi-san had one other trainer, who would be helping us during the tour. We soon got our snow boots, gloves, and instructions on what to do. We were told to lean into the turns and were shown how to operate the brakes. The trainer also taught us a few words to shout out as commands to the dogs, which I promptly forgot. There was a bulletin board with the names and photos of the dogs on our sled team: Vivi,

Kuro, Nami, Mitch, Grizzly, Timber, Kuma, and Diesel, all three to five years old.

During the sledding, Takeshi-san and the other trainer would be following us on a snowmobile to ensure that nothing went disastrously wrong. The two-person sleds were equipped with seats, non-slip standing surfaces, brakes, and anchors. The person in front would be seated while the one in back would be standing. The person in back would be able to step on the brakes—a set of spikes that dug into the ground when you stepped down on them—if necessary. The brakes weren't very impressive looking, so the engineer in me doubted that they would do anything except make an annoying scratching sound. I supposed we could always just jump off into a snowbank if things got out of control. I had no idea how far we would be traveling or how fast a team of eight dogs could pull two adults on a sled. I was about to find out.

As the preparations were being made, the dogs grew visibly and audibly excited. Our anxiety mounted as one of my friends and I boarded the sled and tried to remember what the trainers told us back at the farmhouse. Something about leaning, and some commands to shout out. I wondered if the dogs understood English or only Japanese.

Three...two...one...go! The most surprising aspect was how quiet it all was. Once the dogs started running, they stopped barking and focused all their energy on pulling the sled. Their power was extremely impressive. Our two-passenger sled accelerated with ease and maintained a constant high velocity. We were going, I'd guess, around ten to fifteen miles per hour. Definitely faster than I could run, but not as fast as I could bike on a road. I could see why we were told to lean into the turns, since at such high speeds we could easily have overturned on a tight curve. Luckily there weren't any tight curves, just a wide-open field.

As it turned out, we didn't have to do much on the sled except to hold on. The dogs knew exactly what to do, when to do it, and where to go. We were mere passengers, which was great because it gave us the opportunity to enjoy the environment and to soak in the experience. A fresh coat of powdery snow covered the entire countryside. At least six inches had fallen the night before, giving us a pristine surface to sled on. It also made the sled completely silent while dashing through the snow. During the two-hour tour, we stopped periodically to give the dogs a break, but also to switch around positions on the sled. I even got to ride on the snow mobile with one of the guides.

The hours flew by, and soon we were returning to the farm to say our goodbyes to the dogs. Back inside we were greeted with hot cups of tea and a space heater. It was so cold that we didn't even mind the smell of kerosene as we stripped off our winter gear. Takeshi-san downloaded all the photos and videos he had taken of us, showing us some of the action shots. Not only was he adept at training dogs, he had a good photographic eye as well. We took one final picture: a group shot with all the trainers. I asked Takeshi-san what the local delicacy was, and he quickly recommended a soba restaurant near Shintoku Station. I did not know that this area was known for soba, but I gladly took the advice. A taxi came by to take me and my friends to the restaurant.

A good meal is always a nice way to cap off an adventure, and this time was no different. Sitting in that restaurant with a bowl of hot soba gave us some time to reflect on how fortunate we were to have experienced something so unique and exhilarating that morning. It was definitely the highlight of that trip.

Mushing Works in Shikaoi, Hokkaido

The dogs all seemed healthy and in good spirits.

The sleds

An exhilarating ride

Photo by Takita Takeshi

Video footage can be seen on my YouTube channel: "Adventures with Phil." Subscribe and search for "Dog Sledding in Japan."

Tottori Prefecture
鳥取県

CHAPTER 11
PARAGLIDING OVER SAND DUNES
(パラグライダー)
Tottori Prefecture

Having glided over the snow in Hokkaido, my next adventure took me to Tottori, toward the southern end of Honshu (the main island of Japan), where I would be gliding over the Japan Sea coast while strapped to a wing made of polyester. How better to view Tottori's giant sand dunes than from the air above?

Tottori is the least populated prefecture in all Japan. And there are not that many famous sites to see. This was fine, since I normally look for the not-so-famous places anyway. But since this was going to be my first visit to Tottori, I had to check out the famous Tottori *sakyū* (鳥取砂丘) or sand dunes—a must-see. Still, I wondered how I could make the trip more interesting.

Sometimes I like to open Google Maps and wander around virtually. Whether or not I end up going in person, I like to get a sense of scale, distance, and general directions of landmarks in a new location. Often times I find restaurants with appealing names and other places of interest that I might otherwise never hear about. As I was searching around Tottori on the map, I came across an interesting place called the Tottori Sakyū ParaGlider School. I knew instantly that I had to go.

I was familiar with the sport of paragliding, since some friends of mine were into it, but I had never tried it myself. It seemed thrilling enough while still being relatively safe, so I was hoping for a chance to try it out. I sent an email to the school asking about availability and schedule, but nothing came back. I was a little worried since their website was only in Japanese, and there were no other references to them at other websites like TripAdvisor. Then I saw a link on their website that said, "for tourist – English." Excited, I clicked on the link, which brought up another page with the words, **"Those who cannot speak Japanese at all are not allowed"** in bold print. Damn! With the weekend coming up, this was not looking good.

I was working near Nagoya for two weeks so would have a free weekend to explore. Tottori was a bit far, but still easily reachable by train. I was busy at work that week, working on a prototype ride vehicle for a new upcoming attraction, so was not able to do more research. But my friend Tomomi saved the day by telling me about another paragliding place in Tottori—Zero Paraglider School. I wrote to them and they answered me back immediately via email, in English, and said that it would be no problem and that I would need to bring gloves, for some reason. Tomomi even helped me find a pair of gloves at the 100 Yen (99 cents) store. (Thank you Tomomi-san!)

From Nagoya, it took around three-and-a-half hours to get to Tottori Station by train. From there I took a taxi to the sand dunes.

Sidenote on taxi drivers:
Taxi drivers outside of the major cities in Japan all seem to be over sixty years old, speak no English, and are among the friendliest people I've met anywhere. They talk to me at length in Japanese, even after I tell them in my limited Japanese that I am from America. One driver in Shikoku got his phone out and started using a translation app to tell me things like how he liked Korean dramas and American movies, including his favorite, *Aquaman*. The driver in Tottori asked me if this was my first time there, and if I wanted to pull over at a lookout point to take photos. Never the one to turn down a photo op, I agreed, and he took me on a detour to a hidden spot where I could overlook the sand dunes and the sea beyond. He even got out of the car and offered to take photos of me.

Zero Paraglider School was, of course, just a tour company that gave absolute beginners the opportunity to try paragliding, which was perfect for me. While tandem paragliding allows beginners to fly with an expert, this place only offered singles, so we had to do all the flying ourselves. Being out in the middle of a huge sand pit made this possible. There were no trees or other obstacles to crash into, and the biggest danger was that we would fly over into the sea and land in the waves below, but we were a good distance from the water, so it wasn't a huge concern.

The company was housed in a small building that shared space with a gift shop next door. There were some small lockers for people to leave their valuables, and a table where we signed our lives away (i.e. legal disclaimers). I met my instructor, Yoshi-san, who spoke enough English to guide me as well as two women from Hong Kong. The rest of the group were all young Japanese couples, probably out on dates. I was the oldest person there by far. I should have invited the taxi driver, too!

After a short briefing, we were given paragliders according to our body weight. A paraglider is basically a parachute that is shaped like a wing to produce lift when wind blows across it. By pulling on the nylon cords, you can control the air flow to make turns or to lower gently to the ground. Feeling excited, we donned the huge backpacks and hiked our way out to the sand dunes.

The Tottori sand dunes are over thirty square kilometers in area and are the largest in Japan. Estimated to be 100,000 years old, they are constantly being reshaped by the ever-present wind. This wind is also what makes paragliding possible from such a short height. The tallest dune was probably around 100 to 150 feet tall. That may not sound like much, but having to lug the heavy paraglider in a backpack up that sandy hill before every flight was exhausting. The worst part was the sandy surface, which didn't allow for much traction as we climbed. Instead, our feet just sank into the sand with every step.

Once at the top, we all dropped our backpacks and the instructors helped us remove the contents. The paragliders were made of colorful polyester fabric and had hundreds of nylon cords tied to them. It was a wonder that they weren't just big tangled messes, but the instructors were able to lay the fabric flat with the cords all neatly aligned. Unfolded, my glider was larger than expected, and would be impressive when airborne. Others were already there making flights and the sky was filled with what looked like colorful kites.

Soon it was my time to fly. I stepped into the harness and strapped in. It was like a fall protection harness with loops for your arms and legs which held you securely. Attached to the harness were two bundles of nylon cords, which connected the paraglider to my harness and ended near my head with two hand holds. I was supposed to grip and pull these hand holds during the flight, and the reason why gloves were required. As the excitement mounted, Yoshi-san quickly explained how to fly:

- Both handgrips up allowed for full speed.
- Both hand grips at ear level was for medium speed.
- Both handgrips at shoulder level or below would be the brakes.
- By pulling down with my right hand while keeping the left hand up, would cause me to turn right, and vice versa.

It seemed simple enough, but I still didn't know how I was supposed to get airborne. Well, leave it to the instructors—and the wind. They lifted the paraglider from the ground behind me, and it instantly caught the wind and lifted up above my head. The wind was steady and caused the straps on my chest to pull upward. It wasn't enough to lift me, but I could tell there was a good upward force on the glider. Gripping the hand holds tightly, I started to run. From the top of this hundred-foot-tall sand dune, I ran downhill as fast as I could. After only four or five steps, the ground dropped out beneath me. I was airborne!

It was amazing how quickly and easily I lifted into the air, but there was no time to ponder. My instructor shouted commands to me via a megaphone—to turn right, left, then straight, then turn, etc. My maiden flight didn't last very long. I touched down gently on to the beach far from the water. I was impressed at how smooth it all went and how soft the landing was. With some practice, this could become a nice hobby. But then reality set in—I had to stuff the paraglider into the backpack and carry it up again to the top of the hill, which wasn't so fun.

My next flight was equally exhilarating and pretty soon I found myself getting the hang of it. But as the sand dunes got more crowded with people, including some that were riding camels and others that were "snow" boarding down the sand hills, I had to be careful with my turns and pay more attention to finding a landing spot. Crashing into other people, including our own group members who had just landed, became the biggest safety concern. I didn't want to be the one on the ground who got hit, either, so I had to keep an eye out for all the beginners up in the air once I landed. After a few hours, we'd all gotten multiple flights in (safely), and were ready to head back to the building. The walk back was nice, since it was all downhill, but also because it gave some time to reflect over the day's activities.

Seeing a beautiful landscape like the Tottori sand dunes was great but experiencing it while gliding through the air gave a better perspective. The overall size of the sand dunes was more easily visible from the air, and I left with a better appreciation of the enormous forces of nature that created them. I could see why they took thousands of years to form and was happy to spend an afternoon looking down from above.

Tottori Sand Dunes

One of the beginners getting help from instructors

A paraglider about to take off

Gorgeous scenery

The people in the distance provide a sense of scale.

Ehime Prefecture
愛媛県

CHAPTER 12
ISLAND HOPPING ON A BICYCLE:
THE SHIMANAMI KAIDO (しまなみ海道)
Hiroshima to Ehime Prefecture

It was an epic road trip. Seventy kilometers of stunning seaside roads, six islands via six bridges and a ferry crossing, and an overnight stay at a traditional Japanese house—all done from the seat of a bicycle. The Shimanami Kaido is part of the Nishiseto Expressway connecting Hiroshima Prefecture on Honshu to Ehime Prefecture on Shikoku (the largest and smallest of the four main Japanese islands, respectively). The route is notable for having a clearly marked bike path along its entire length, with dedicated bike lanes in many of the areas.

Starting in Onomichi City on the Hiroshima side, the bike path connects the six small islands in the Seto Inland Sea: Mukaishima, Innoshima, Ikuchijima, Omishima, Hakatajima and Oshima, before ending in Imabari City in Ehime. (If you hadn't guessed, *shima* and *jima* mean island in Japanese.) At around twenty years old, the bike paths and bridges are modern and very well maintained. Several small towns, more than 150 bicycle-friendly restaurants, repair shops, guest houses, and other facilities (i.e. restrooms) cater to the cyclists passing by. But strangely enough, the road doesn't feel "touristy," inauthentic, or overcrowded. Rather, it somehow maintains the look and feel of small-town Japan.

Our journey started in Tokyo. After a week-long session of meetings and many hours sitting in a conference room, my friends and I were excited to head out Friday after work. John, Eddy, Rick, and I took the Shinkansen to Shin-Onomichi, Hiroshima. Eating *ekiben* (駅弁), railway bento, for dinner on the train, we arrived four-and-a-half hours later and checked into our hotel well past midnight. I fell asleep soon thereafter, only to be awakened at 3 a.m. by a huge thunderstorm. Oh great, I thought, that should make for an interesting bike ride. I suppose we went prepared for foul weather since it is so common in that area, but, still, rain is never that welcome on a weekend getaway.

Thankfully the morning brought clear skies, and although the weather was a bit chilly, we were eager to start the adventure. The trip would take around ten hours at typical bicycling speeds, but we were planning to take frequent breaks for sightseeing and photography. After breakfast at the hotel, we made our way to the local bike rental shops.

Random sidenote:
When renting the bikes, we had to fill in an application form which listed several requirements. Things like: we had to have picture IDs, we had to be in good health, we had to not be under the influence of alcohol, etc. Halfway through the list I noticed the requirement of "no tattoos allowed." As silly as this may sound to westerners, this is a common requirement in Japan, where tattoos are still taboo and a sign of the *yakuza* or organized crime groups. Many places such as fitness gyms and *onsen* (hot springs) will not allow anyone with a tattoo, and I even saw this rule at Nagashima Spaland, one of the largest amusement

parks in Japan. Why criminals would want to draw attention to themselves with large tattoos is still a mystery to me, and perhaps the topic of a future research trip. Thankfully, many places are relaxing this rule, especially for foreigners who are obviously not part of the *yakuza*. But as for renting bikes, tattoos were still not allowed. Luckily there were no strip searches.

The bike shop was huge. Located on the first floor of a parking garage, they had a hundred bikes all lined up for us to choose from. Bikes of all sizes and shapes, from mountain bikes to cruisers. We could even try them out first and pedal around the garage before making the final selection. Helmets were included, and once we had everything selected, we were all set for the two-day journey.

The first island on the route would be Mukaishima. While a road bridge exists from Onomichi to Mukaishima, it does not have a dedicated bike lane, so many riders prefer the ferry. Conveniently enough, the ferry harbor was located just behind the hotel, so my friends and I, along with about twenty other cyclists packed into the ferry and made our way across the narrow straight. Once off the ferry, we looked for the blue line on the road that would mark the next seventy kilometers of our journey.

After biking through the island via an unremarkable path, we soon came upon the first bridge, the Innoshima Bridge. A strikingly beautiful, 770-meter long suspension bridge, it connects Mukaishima to Innoshima, and would be our first real challenge. Large suspension bridges like the Innoshima need to be very high above water to allow for ship traffic to pass below. That means that in order to bike across it, we first had to get up to the bridge level, which entailed biking up a steep incline. Having a dedicated bike road that wound its way up to the bridge helped, but it was still an exhausting ride especially while carrying everything for a two-day trip on our bikes. I was glad that I had chosen a premium road bike. It did cost more, but the lightweight frame, narrow road tires, and the additional gears paid off on the steep inclines. Once we made it up, we were rewarded with a spectacular view of the Seto Inland Sea and the nearby islands. The multi-decked bridge had an entire level just for bikes and pedestrians, so it was an easy cross to the next island.

We stopped frequently along the way: for lunch, for gelato, and for photos and drone videos. We slowly continued making our way across the islands. Every bridge was as challenging as the first, especially as we were getting more and more tired through the day, but I didn't mind. The scenery kept getting more and more beautiful as we went further into the chain of islands.

We finally made it to Oshima Island, where we were going to stop for the night, after seven hours of biking. We had found a place online—a renovated, hundred-year-old traditional Japanese house called Ogata House. Ogata House is now a guest house run by its owner, Makiko-san, who purchased and renovated the property a few years ago. She had lived and attended college in the United States so spoke English very well. (I would highly recommend staying there during any visits to that area.) The hospitality, scenery, and tranquility there were second to none.

Prior to dinner, Makiko-san served us tea and some light snacks to get our appetites going. We sat on the back patio and watched the beautiful Seto Inland Sea. The discussion soon turned to dinner, and how we should get there. No one wanted to get back onto a bicycle. Fortunately, Makiko-san called us a taxi. Being off the main roads, there weren't any restaurants within walking distance. Plus, it was pitch dark at night with very little street lighting, so biking or walking around was not recommended. If it wasn't for the cloud cover, it would have been a spectacularly starry night.

Makiko-san recommended a restaurant called *Tanpopo* on nearby Hakata Island, and unlike in the 1985 film of the same name, this place was not a ramen joint. Instead it was an okonomiyaki[6] place serving some of the best Hiroshima-style okonomiyaki I'd had in a long time. (That's the kind with yakisoba noodles inside the pancake along with the usual cabbage, pork, and seafood). Despite the complete lack of English, we managed to order our food and drinks and even asked for a taxi to return home. Maybe my Japanese was getting better?

I awoke the next morning to a lovely sunrise. Being on the east coast of Oshima Island, we got a clear view of the rising sun over the sea. Still a bit sore from the day before, I walked around the property and took in the fresh morning air. We had biked most of the way to our destination on the first day so thought that we could relax and take it easy on the second. Little did we know that the worst was yet to come.

After leaving Ogata House, we rejoined the Shimanami Kaido by following the ever-present blue line on the road. The six kilometers of road that cut through the middle of the island felt like the steepest stretch road ever paved. It eventually led to the highest and longest bridge on the tour, the Kurushima Kaikyo Bridge. Stretching over four kilometers, the bridge itself seemed like a never-ending incline, and offered little to no protection from the wind, which made pedaling that much more difficult. (Why was the wind always in our face and slowing us down? I found out later that the prevailing winds were from west to east, so maybe we should have biked in the other direction.) To my tired old legs, it felt like the Pyrenees Stage of the Tour de France.

---

[6] Okonomiyaki is a savory pancake containing cabbage, seafood, and pork, fried on a pan. It is then topped with special sauces and mayonnaise. Originating in Osaka, it is one of the signature dishes of the Kansai region.

After the bridge was a nice gentle downhill all the way to our destination, Imabari City, in Ehime Prefecture, which we reached after a total of four hours of biking that day. We quickly found the bike shops and returned our (one-way) rentals. Running a bit ahead of schedule, we took the two-hour train to Okayama and had a quick lunch. I picked up some *kibi-dango* (specialty sweet dumplings from Okayama) as *omiyage* (gifts) and got on the four-hour Shinkansen back to Tokyo. It was another long day of travel.

Having only a weekend away from Tokyo, this was a tough trip to squeeze in, and we were not able to explore the islands as fully as I would have liked. Nevertheless, it was a spectacularly picturesque, breathtakingly beautiful, and immensely challenging and satisfying trip, and being on a multi-day bicycle voyage really brought a sense of being close to nature. Although I was never that far away from a convenience store or a taxicab, I still felt like we had ventured out into the wilderness with only the supplies on our backs. It was an epic road trip, and one of the best experiences I had had in all of Japan.

Selecting bikes at the rental shop

Innoshima Bridge

Dedicated bike lanes along the Seto Inland Sea

Hataka Oshima Bridge, heading to Oshima Island

Ogata House on Oshima Island

Our beautiful rooms

Okonomiyaki (Hiroshima style)

The Kurushima Kaikyo Bridge: 4.1 km long,
composed of three suspension bridges in a row.

The route taken

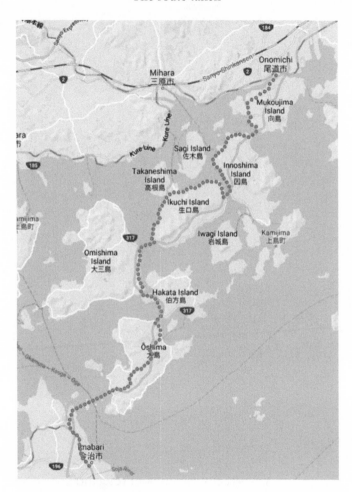

Video of the trip can be seen on my YouTube channel: "Adventures with Phil." Subscribe and search for "Shimanami Kaido."

Yamanashi and Shizuoka Prefectures
山梨県　静岡県

CHAPTER 13
CLIMBING MT. FUJI (富士山)
Yamanashi and Shizuoka Prefectures

You can't discuss nature in Japan without talking about the cultural and geological giant that is Mt. Fuji. Ever present in the Japanese landscape, on clear days it can easily be seen from downtown Tokyo a hundred kilometers away. Mt. Fuji is more than just the highest mountain in Japan, it is a cultural icon deeply rooted in Shinto mythology and was considered sacred for centuries. A major influence on Japanese art and literature, it became a UNESCO World Heritage Cultural Site more recently and remains cherished just the same.

To climb it is a rite of passage for many school children and families alike, but also a celebration of longevity as more than 2,000 people aged seventy or above climb Mt. Fuji every year. In 2017, a ninety-three-year-old man named Toyoda Masashi, became the oldest person to climb Mt. Fuji that year, just beating out six others who were also over ninety years old. The oldest ever is believed to have been a 103-year-old man.[7]

---

[7] Japan Times, March 26, 2018.

Fuji is essentially a steep hike. It doesn't require any technical mountaineering skills, but with a hiking distance of over eleven miles, and an elevation gain of almost 5,000 feet, the climb is strenuous, especially on the loose, gravel-like surface that is common on the trails. There's a Japanese saying that goes something like this, "A person that never climbs Mt. Fuji even once is a fool, but a person that climbs more than once is a bigger fool." Well, I am secure enough with my foolishness to tell you that I have climbed Mt. Fuji. Twice.

So why spend eighteen hours outside in the cold and go through eleven hours of arduous hiking for a second time? Well, because the first time around I did not get to see the goraikō (御来光) or the "arrival of light." To see the sun rising over the "Land of the Rising Sun" from its tallest peak was high on my bucket list. Unfortunately, the first time around, my friends Andres, Kris, Jon, and I were met by a typhoon bringing heavy rain and forty-mile-per-hour winds to the summit. At times, the wind blew so strongly that I had to get down on all fours and crawl. Fortunately, we had reserved space at a mountain hut near the summit, which allowed us to take shelter for a few hours, and even have some curry rice.

The plan was to sleep for a couple of hours in the hut and then head to the summit for the sunrise, but the only thing we got were howling winds all night long. At one point, I was genuinely worried that the roof of the wooden structure would fly away. I don't know how much sleep I got that night, but it wasn't much. Soon the time came to pack up and head to the summit. As soon as I exited the hut, I realized that I couldn't see ten feet ahead of me, much less the summit. Forget the sunrise. We were completely fogged in. But at least the rain had stopped, so my friends and I made our way slowly to the summit and took selfies with a cloudy background. The sun had already risen by that point, but we could barely tell.

As grueling as that experience was, we were ready for the challenge of another climbing season the following year. We were confident we'd get better weather, since it certainly couldn't get worse. Almost exactly a year later, I was back at the foot of Mt. Fuji. Joining me again were Kris and Andres, along with two newcomers, Janice and Jenny. A little more prepared and experienced, we set out for the climb on an ominously overcast day. We were going to climb up the Yoshida Trail on the northeast side and descend on the Fujinomiya Trail on the south side of the mountain. Each trail is divided into approximately ten stations, with the first station, at sea level, being the lowest and tenth being on the summit. Roads and buses go up to the fifth station on each trail, and this is where almost everyone starts their climb. The station has now become a large tourist facility with shops and restaurants. Non-climbers also take the buses up to the fifth station to be on the mountain without any physical exertion. I don't even know if the stations lower than the fifth still exist, but I have heard of people climbing the entire mountain starting from sea level. I didn't have time nor the desire for that during a weekend away from work. The fifth station on the Yoshida Trail is at an elevation of 7,562 feet and that's where we started our climb to the summit at 12,388 feet.

After fueling up with some ramen at the fifth station, we started our hike on the foggy trail. The early portion of the trail was gently sloped, wide open, and lined with lots of vegetation and trees. The ground was a gravel-like texture composed of small black rocks, which created a slippery footing. Occasional breaks in the fog gave us a view of the valley below. It was summertime down there and looked nice and warm. We pressed on upward into the clouds.

It started to rain almost right away. The light sprinkle turned into larger droplets. Andres immediately pulled out a pair of ski goggles and put them on. He had remembered the pelting rain and wind from the previous year and had come prepared. I tried to pack as light as possible, remembering something else from the previous year: my aching back. But I had also come prepared, with ibuprofen. Thankfully, the rain soon stopped and gave us a chance to take photos before sunset.

We had reserved space at a mountain hut this time around as well, but it was near the bottom of the trail and not the top. All the others were already sold out, so we were forced to stop for the night much earlier than desired. Our place was the Hinode-kan Mountain Hut at the seventh station, at an elevation of 8,858 feet. It had only taken us an hour to get there, so the bulk of the climbing was still facing us the next day, or rather later that night. We knew we had another six to eight hours of climbing, depending on weather conditions, so we were planning to head out again at around 8 p.m. This gave us time to eat (curry rice again) and use the crude restrooms.

The "sleeping" area was a series of bunks arranged in long rows like in a train. This being Japan, everyone took off their shoes to enter the sleeping area, which kept the floor clean, but made the entire area stink like everyone's wet hiking boots! What a nasty odor. I came close to vomiting. It didn't help that I had just inhaled a bowl of curry rice, so I just dropped off my backpack and went back outside for some fresh air and to get a stamp for my hiking stick.

Sidenote on Fuji hiking sticks:
One cool souvenir to get during the climb is a hiking stick. Made of plain, unfinished wood, you can get special stamps burned into the wood at all the stations along the climb. The stamps are all different, with some having the station names and elevations, while others have simple artwork like an image of Mt. Fuji. Collecting all the stamps will result in an impressive looking staff covered

---

with memories, branded into the wood. (Be sure to bring a lot of 100 Yen coins, for these stamps as well as the bathrooms.)

After getting my stamp, I took a deep breath and went back into the sleeping quarters. Our reserved sleeping space, for five people, was no more than ten feet wide, if that. As someone who moves around a lot during sleep, I felt bad for whoever would end up next to me that night. I was tired but not tired enough to sleep much, plus it was only 6 p.m. anyway. The plan was to get as much rest as possible before heading to the summit during the night. In order to see the sunrise from the summit, people often climb the mountain all night long and hope that the weather is clear at the peak. I suppose the frequent foul weather at Fuji is what makes a clear sunrise so famously elusive. After maybe thirty minutes of sleep, I gave up and went outside again. It was fully dark now and I could see a long line of headlamps as people started the climb from below. The tiny specs of light flickering in the distance outlined the steep slope of the mountain and showed how far up we were. The Yoshida Trail, being the most popular, can resemble a queue line at Disneyland. Time to get moving, I thought.

At 8 p.m., we left the hut for the summit, and after two hours we reached the eighth station. It was much slower going now in the darkness. The landscape was barren of any trees or vegetation which gave free reign to the wind. The cold wind picked up, but as long as we kept moving, it was not too bad. Keep moving, I kept thinking to myself. But as the trail got narrower and more crowded, it became difficult to keep moving. Sometimes I was only able to take a single step and had to wait several seconds for the person in front of me to move. It got ridiculously close to being a conga line—a slow, freezing cold, music-less conga line in the pitch-black landscape. Good thing we left early.

Two-and-a-half grueling hours later, we reached the next station—the ninth. We wanted to rest and warm up, but noticed that the higher we went, the more crowded the trail got. So, we kept moving. Remarkably, as crowded as it was, everyone was dead silent. There were no discussions going on. No small talk. No mood for banter. At that height—over 10,000 feet—all I could hear was the wind buffeting my hoodie and my own labored breathing. *Why am I breathing so loudly?* I thought. *I hoped that no one else can hear it. Two thousand more feet to climb.*

The thinning air was taking a toll. With ever decreasing amounts of oxygen in the air, physical exertion was becoming more difficult. The year before, I had visited Tibet and had gone up to 17,000 feet with no ill effects. But I wasn't climbing a mountain then. Still, I was lucky that I didn't suffer from altitude sickness, and that, here, I was doing ok so far. Almost there. Time was moving slowly. Instead of seconds and minutes, all I had keeping time were footsteps. *Just put one step in front of the other,* is all I could think about. The small pebbles in my shoes, which had been constantly bothering me for the past four hours, were now helping to remind me that I was continuing to take steps. As my feet went numb from the cold, I needed the pebbles to tell me that my feet were still alive. *One step in front of the other. One step in front of the other.*

All of a sudden, the trail leveled off, and I found myself in a small clearing. I saw a manmade structure and realized that we had finally made it. We were on the summit! It was around three in the morning, a full seven hours since we'd left the mountain hut. We were relieved to have arrived, but unfortunately the sun wouldn't rise for another two hours at 5:11 a.m., and we were at what felt like the coldest and windiest spot in all of Japan.

As the summit became packed with people, a huge line formed to get into the final mountain station—a small hut that serves instant ramen and even has a vending machine. Only in Japan! The main draw, of course, was to get out of the freezing cold, so they were limiting the number of people allowed to enter as well as the time spent inside. With nothing better to do, we got in line and waited. After an hour or so, we got into what felt like heaven. Not only was the instant warmth nice, but the instant ramen was the best thing I had tasted in a long time. And to top it all off, we got some hot corn soup in a can! After warming my hands on the small can, I opened up the sweet smelling, mouth-watering, thick corn potage, and it was amazing. I could have stayed there all day. Forget the sunrise, just give me more corn soup. But alas, our time to leave came soon and as I stepped outdoors, the cold air hit my face like a bucket of ice water. Within seconds, the warmth of the hut was a distant memory, and my friends and I huddled together in the cold to wait for the rising sun.

The distant lights of Tokyo and Yokohama were clearly visible. That was a good sign, because it meant that the day would be clear. As the sky slowly brightened, dark shades of blue turned into cyan and then to orange. The orange was at first just along the horizon, until it became brighter and brighter and filled the sky. The Kanagawa coastline could now be seen with the Pacific Ocean in the distance, and then suddenly it came. A bright solar flare broke above the eastern horizon and instantly illuminated the sky. An audible gasp could be heard from the assembled crowd, as camera shutters fired off in rapid succession. As exciting as that moment was, I felt tranquil as we were all filled with a sense of awe and beauty. I no longer noticed the cold.

Several minutes passed. The crowd started to thin. Some went back into the hut, while most of the others started the hike down the mountain. Since we were descending on the other side, we started our hike along the rim of the volcano to get to the south face. With the last eruption in 1707, Fuji is still considered an active volcano. The caldera at the summit forms a deep pit with a cone inside the crater rim. Looking like a photo from Mars, the unearthly landscape was filled with reddish boulders on top of gravel layers of gray and brown. I wondered what it might be like during an eruption (assuming I wasn't instantly vaporized). The view of lava flowing out of this crater and down the mountain slope would be formidable and terrifying.

Soon, we got to the south side and started our descent. The hike down was in some ways more difficult and dangerous. While the climb up was slow and steady, the descent was fast and, at times, uncontrolled. The loose gravel surface made finding sure footing difficult, so we had to be careful to control our speed. Having the hiking stick helped, and I used it like a ski pole as I navigated the moguls of volcanic rock below me. Descending used a different set of muscles as new parts of my body started to ache. I was definitely going to be sore for several days thereafter. Good thing I had more ibuprofen.

Overall the descent took about three hours, and we were soon back in the warm summer air. With a huge sense of achievement and relief, I emptied my shoes of dust and pebbles and sat down for the first time in what seemed like days. Although the goal was to see the sunrise, accomplishing the climb itself was the most satisfying achievement. The spectacular sunrise was just the cherry on top of a face-to-face encounter with nature and with ourselves. Mt. Fuji draws throngs of tourists every year, but it is still a magnificent sight to be seen and should be climbed at least once in a lifetime. Maybe even twice.

At the base of Mt. Fuji (started off with clear skies)

At the summit during a typhoon (first climb)

Photo by Kris Laffin

Starting the climb on the Yoshida Trail (second climb)

Our sleeping quarters at the seventh station

Curry rice for dinner at the mountain hut

Getting souvenir stamps burnt into my hiking stick

So happy indoors with hot corn soup

Photo by Jenny McGowan

Land of the Rising Sun

Spectacular view

The volcanic caldera at the peak

Toyama Prefecture
富山県

CHAPTER 14
LOCKED OUT IN KUROBE GORGE
(黒部峡谷)
Toyama Prefecture

Sometimes nothing goes right. I caught a late Shinkansen out of Tokyo after work ran long on a Friday night. I just managed to make my connection in Toyama Prefecture, at a tiny station called Shin-Kurobe. From there I took the oldest train I've ever seen in Japan: a diesel engine with a single car and conductor that had to come out of the cab at each stop to collect cash from the passengers as they disembarked. As the few passengers slowly departed one by one, I remained all alone on the train as it headed deep into the night. The train finally arrived at the terminal just before midnight, where I paid the conductor in coins and stepped out into the cold. It was late June, but the heat of Tokyo was long gone, replaced by cold, foggy mountain air. I was at Unazukionsen, the end of the line and the entrance to Kurobe Gorge.

I knew I was going to get in late, so I had mapped out the location of my hotel in case I needed to walk. Sure enough, the station was deserted when I arrived: no taxis, no buses, no people. The hotel shuttle bus had stopped running hours earlier, and there was not a soul in sight. Wow, I thought, this was a resort town? The hotel I had reserved was a huge complex with an *onsen* and, supposedly, a spectacular view of Kurobe Gorge. I headed out into the dark unable to see anything.

The hotel was less than a mile away, but it turned out to be a mile uphill. To make things worse, it started to rain. It was just a sprinkle, but it was still annoying as I trekked toward the hotel with a heavy backpack. In about forty-five minutes, I crested the hill and saw a large building just a few yards away. Google Maps identified it as the Hotel Kurobe, my final destination for the night. It was a large building all right, but something was amiss. It was *completely* dark. No signs, no streetlights, no light from any of the windows, nothing. It looked abandoned, like something out of a Stephen King movie. Getting a little worried, I walked up to the automatic sliding front door. I got to about a yard away and nothing happened. I waved my arms, but still nothing. I looked through the glass and all I could see was one dimly lit lamp at the front desk; a front desk that was devoid of any people. In fact, the entire lobby was deserted, and for all I knew the entire town was abandoned.

Not wanting to stand out in the cold rain, I called the hotel's phone number only to get a message in Japanese. I looked on my phone for other hotels in the area, but nothing close came up, and those would probably be deserted as well, since this seemed to be the largest hotel in the area. So, I did what any engineer would do: I broke in. I knew that the automatic doors would have a manual override in case of fires, so I stuck my fingers into the gap and pulled one of the doors until it slid open enough for me to squeeze through. Whew, at least I was out of the rain. The large lobby had several sofas and chairs spread out, but there was still no one in sight. I almost wished that I had set off an alarm and that security would show up, but there was nothing but utter silence.

The lone lamp at the front desk made for a spooky mood. If I had not been so tired, I would have been terrified. But I had a challenge ahead of me, so I didn't have time to be scared. I called the hotel again, and the desk phone in front of me rang. No wonder I got a message earlier. This time I listened to the message carefully to see if I could pick anything up. Nothing. It was way too fast. But then at the end, the voice listed out several numbers. Aha! I could understand numbers, and those were probably a phone number to call, maybe for an after-hours desk. I got a pen and paper and started writing down the numbers. The message was spoken so fast that I had to call back three times to get all the numbers right, but I eventually got it. I was feeling quite proud of myself as I dialed what was clearly an alternate phone number. Ring, ring… it was the same desk phone in front of me.

Noooooo!!! After calming down, I decided to look around the front desk to see if I could see my name anywhere, maybe with a key. After all, not only did I have a reservation, I had pre-paid for the room as well. But I saw nothing. Everything had been neatly put away for the night. I won't say that I rifled through the desk or anything, but I may have looked around a little. All I saw of note was a stack of small towels on a shelf off to the side. Of course! They have an *onsen*, and these must be towels they give to guests as they check in, or something like that. After all that had happened, soaking in a nice hot *onsen* sounded spectacular. I grabbed a towel and went searching the building.

The hotel was huge, with multiple wings and more than ten floors, but appeared to be completely empty. As I walked up and down the corridors and the stairs, it felt eerily, again, like I'd booked a room at the hotel from *The Shining*. If I had seen a pair of twin girls then, I would have freaked out. Thankfully, no one was awake at 2 a.m. I finally found the *onsen* in the basement level, and to my great relief it was open 24 hours. I would have broken in anyway, but it was nice that I didn't have to. At least one thing went right. There was also a large bathroom nearby, so I had all the amenities of a resort—except for a room and a bed.

Fortunately, the *onsen* was magnificent. After showering, which in itself was sensational, I stepped into the hot pool and just felt all the stress dissolve away. There were no more worries, and I could have just sat there all night long. From being cold and scared to feeling complete relaxation—oh, it was all worth it, almost. I don't remember how long I stayed, but I was getting sleepy, so I dried myself off and got dressed. I was so tired that I was ready to sleep on anything, so I headed back to the lobby and selected one of the many sofas in the area. Not bad. There was an area off to the side, with a sofa and a coffee table and a power outlet, so I made myself at home.

I didn't sleep long as the rising sun really lit up the place. With no one in sight yet, I got up and cleaned up the area and waited for the hotel staff to show up. Since I had already paid for the room, I wanted, at least, to see it, and to sleep some more. At around 6 a.m. I finally saw people. An elderly man walked around the lobby. Then another person who looked to be in his seventies came strolling through. The hotel staff finally showed up and started preparing the front desk. There was a young woman and a middle-aged man who were in for a surprise. I waited a few minutes and then walked up to the woman to check in. The look on her face was that of utter confusion. Where did this person come from? How did he get here so early in the morning? It was long before the trains started running. Why was he so disheveled? I could almost see the thought bubbles forming above her head like in a *manga* comic book. I waited as she slowly checked for my reservation. Her mind was definitely distracted, and after what seemed like an hour, she finally found my name, checked me in, and gave me my key. I don't know if she figured out what had happened, but the look of confusion was still on her face as I walked away.

The room was, indeed, very nice, and as promised there a striking view of the gorge and river below. Later that day, I planned to hike in the gorge itself, but for now I just wanted to sleep. At that very moment, the futon on the tatami mat floor was the most desirable thing in the world to me. I fell fast asleep.

After a few hours I awoke and decided I could still make the most out of the remaining day. I was there to see the famed Kurobe Gorge, one of the deepest canyons in Japan. To enter the gorge, I decided to ride the Kurobe Gorge Railway, a sightseeing train originally built to support the construction of the Kurobe Dam. I caught one of the afternoon trains and took the winding, twenty-kilometer route from Unazuki to Keyakidaira station. The scenic, eighty-minute journey led me deep into the gorge, over twenty bridges, through forty tunnels, and offered picturesque views of the gorge below. The gorge walls were steep with traces of snow clinging on from the previous winter and melting into emerald colored waters below. Further in the canyon, I could see pools of natural hot springs steaming in the distance.

I disembarked at Keyakidaira station—the end of the line. From there, I hiked along the Kurobe River, getting close enough to get my feet wet on many occasions. Although it was summer, the temperature inside the gorge was nice and cool. River rapids generated mist enveloping parts of the trail in fog, making for a refreshing escape from the summer heat. Despite the screw-up the night before, I had a wonderful time in Kurobe Gorge. It was a relaxing getaway from busy Tokyo.

Endnote: I later found out that I was supposed to call ahead and make arrangements to check-in after 11 p.m. Good to know for next time.

The beautiful Hotel Kurobe

The lobby where I slept

My eventual room

The spectacular view from my room

Taking the Kurobe Gorge Railway

Beautiful emerald waters

Inside Kurobe Gorge

Kurobe River

The great outdoors are not far no matter where you are in Japan. For more getaways into nature, visit these places:

- Yakushima Island in Kagoshima – to hike in the dense forest that inspired the movie, *Princess Mononoke*.

- Aokigahara Forest and Ice Caves in Yamanashi – to hike in the "sea of trees" and to explore the caves that stay freezing cold year-round.

- Canyoning in Gunma – to rappel down cliffs and waterfalls.

- Cherry Blossoms at Hirosaki Castle in Aomori – one of the most beautiful sites to see the annual cherry blossoms.

- Koyasan in Wakayama – to visit ancient Buddhist monasteries and temples deep in the forest.

- Mt. Shirouma including the Daisekkei Snow Gorge in Nagano – to climb the Japanese Alps.

PART V
WHEN NATURE STRIKES

Japan is no stranger to natural disasters: seasonal typhoons, erupting volcanoes, and rattling earthquakes are all common here, and have been throughout history. The Japanese people have had to face many catastrophes and have shown incredible strength in their ability to recover and carry on. I believe this adversity has strengthened the culture and has given the nation the will to plan ahead against future disasters. It has also given the people the power to endure unimaginable tragedies.

There have been efforts to mitigate these disasters with a lot of planning and forethought. Some attempts have worked flawlessly, while others have not. One example of an ingenious endeavor is a massive public project that has solved the problems of devastating floods in the Kanto Plain near Tokyo. Unfortunately, other examples have shown that mother nature can't always be tamed completely. On one March day in 2011, she struck with one of the largest natural disasters in modern history. Even in a country as well prepared as Japan, the Tohoku earthquake and subsequent tsunami quickly overwhelmed all man-made protective measures previously put in place. Measures, that were supposed to control and prevent large-scale damage, but instead allowed unthinkable destruction and loss of life across the country.

Saitama Prefecture
埼玉県

CHAPTER 15
UNDERGROUND CATHEDRAL:
THE METROPOLITAN AREA
OUTER UNDERGROUND DISCHARGE
CHANNEL (首都圏外郭放水路)
Saitama Prefecture

If I told you that a drainage canal was a tourist attraction, you may think that I have finally run out of places to visit in Japan. On the contrary, I'd been trying to get to the Metropolitan Area Outer Underground Discharge Channel in Saitama for years! Unfortunately, the site is difficult to reach for foreign visitors as it requires a car to make the one-hour trip from Tokyo, as there are no train stations nearby. Rental cars are available, but the right-handed steering wheels and left-side of the road driving make it an uneasy venture for most westerners. The tours also require that someone in your group speaks Japanese. All of which means that the visit must be carefully planned.

With a heavy rainy season, the area around Tokyo is hit with damaging floods every year. In an effort to alleviate the damage, engineers built a massive flood control channel to combat mother nature. Located deep underneath the fields of Saitama, the project is an engineering marvel on a scale like nothing else I've seen. The purpose of the channel is to relieve the flood plains near the Naka and Ayase River basins, and to drain the excess water into the much larger Edogawa River via an underground channel. The channel is four miles long with five gigantic drainage banks, each over 100 feet in diameter and 220 feet deep. These banks collect the flood waters and direct them into the underground channel. The channel then flows the water into a reservoir tank where four powerful pumps release the water into the Edogawa River. It all sounds simple enough on paper, where the scale is less clear. The only way to properly appreciate it is to visit for yourself, which I finally got to do on an early December afternoon when one of my friends in Japan offered to drive me and a few others there *and* be our requisite Japanese speaker.

The tour started with a view of the control room. With several monitors and computer stations, it resembled a small version of NASA's Mission Control. Then we got a quick briefing and were given badges to wear during the tour. (They also had an app that you could use during the tour for more information and some fun photo effects, but I didn't bother with it.) After this first part, we walked outside and headed to a soccer field. At the end of the field was a small concrete blockhouse with a single door and no windows. There were around forty people on the tour that day so there was no way that we could all fit into that concrete structure, but the guide opened the door anyway.

The door led to a staircase heading deep underground. We entered and started climbing down the stairs. There were signs saying "no photos allowed on the stairs" so we just kept descending, down the stairs, an endless progression of steps, to a landing, then a U-turn and more steps down. Back and forth, I don't know how many times, until we finally reached the bottom.

We were inside the reservoir tank! A gigantic room made entirely of concrete, over three football fields in size. I could barely see the other end of this massive cavern, and you could easily drive a car inside this space. A series of temple-like columns supported the roof high above us, and large lighting fixtures shined down from above. Affectionately called the "Cathedral," it reminded me of the majestic, medieval churches of Europe—not as ornate, perhaps, but way more badass. The tank, we learned, can hold 248,508 cubic meters or 66 million gallons of water, which is the equivalent to a hundred Olympic-sized swimming pools. The sheer scale of this volume was difficult to get my mind around, but when one of the guides walked away into the distance, I immediately got a sense of dimensions. She looked to be the size of an insect compared to the vast open space surrounding us. Connected to this tank were four massive pumps—powered by a 1400 horsepower jet turbine engine—that could fill an Olympic-sized swimming pool in twelve seconds. It was disappointing that they were not in operation that day. Of course, we couldn't have been in the tank if the system were running.

One of the five drainage banks, which collected water from the area above and fed into the cathedral, stood at the end of the cavern. Going even deeper into the ground, the hundred-foot-wide pit did have some muddy water below, giving a hint of what it might be like during a flood. Looking down two-hundred feet into that staggering abyss, my friend remarked that it was like looking into *jigoku,* or hell itself.

As we climbed back up the stairs, I kept looking back to see if I could get a panoramic view of the entire site. Stopping for a brief moment, I looked down and saw the area where we had just stood. It looked like a tiny patch of dirt in a gigantic stadium. The immense scale of it all was astonishing.

As an engineer, I was having a hard time believing that something like this was actually built. To construct this above ground would have been a Herculean feat, but to do it all underground was unfathomable. Having worked on some large construction sites myself, I was imagining all the planning and labor that would have gone into this project, not to mention the headaches. Technical challenges aside, the cost of this project must have been astronomical, while the benefits to society were not immediately tangible. Sure, it eliminated the flooding that sometimes occurred in this area, but it must have taken a lot of long-term commitments and steadfast political will to get it done. I kept thinking that there was no way something like this could be built in modern-day America, with our short attention spans and general disdain for large public projects. Yet this type of forward planning and public works project is exactly in the Japanese spirit of doing something for the greater good, where individuals pitch in to build something to benefit society as a whole. Being completely underground, the system did not disrupt the natural landscape. It is not only a great work of engineering, but an example of design that maintains harmony with nature.

A diagram of the overall system

The entrance to the underground cathedral

Inside the underground cathedral (reservoir tank)

One of the five drainage banks
(see the handrails on the upper right for scale)

Immense columns

Fukushima Prefecture
福島県

CHAPTER 16
NUCLEAR MELTDOWN:
THE TOHOKU EARTHQUAKE
AND TSUNAMI
Fukushima Prefecture

The area was a ghost town, a post-apocalyptic landscape from a Hollywood movie. Everything in the Fukushima nuclear exclusion zone—rubble from the earthquake, abandoned cars, and deserted buildings—seemed to be frozen in time. You could practically feel the urgency of the people as they dropped everything and fled. Maybe they thought that the evacuation was temporary, but as of yet, no one has returned.

Special permission was required to enter the area. We had to have pre-arranged authorization forms and had to show our passports to the guards patrolling the perimeter. We also got personal radiation detectors to measure the total dosage that we would receive on the tour. With everything in order, our vehicle slowly drove past the gates. The already serious mood in the vehicle got even more somber. What did I get myself into?

On March 11, 2011, Japan changed forever. At 2:46

p.m. a 9.1-magnitude earthquake hit off the north eastern shore of Japan. It shook the country for more than six minutes and became the most powerful earthquake ever recorded in Japan. The unprecedented catastrophe that resulted came in three stages: the earthquake, which caused a tsunami, which caused a nuclear disaster at the Fukushima Daiichi Nuclear Plant.

The earthquake was so powerful that it actually moved the entire island of Honshu with its 104 million residents about eight feet to the east and changed the earth's rotational axis by four inches.[8] Think of the force required to move basically an entire nation by eight feet in just a few minutes. What would happen if your house was jolted and dragged eight feet? Would there be anything left?

More than most nations, Japan is accustomed to and prepared for earthquakes, which are common in the area. But a 9.1 quake is something else. The Tohoku earthquake was the fourth most powerful earthquake ever recorded in history. The energy released by the Tohoku earthquake was calculated to be equivalent to the energy used by the entire city of Los Angeles in a whole year. And all that released in just six minutes.

The devastation left by the quake was tempered only by the fact that it was centered forty-three miles out at sea. But this, of course, made things worse to come, as the quake thrusted a 110-mile-wide section of seabed up by twenty-five feet, creating a massive tsunami, spreading out all over the Pacific Ocean.

The north east prefectures facing the Pacific took the brunt of the tsunami. Iwate, Miyagi, and Fukushima prefectures saw waves over twenty-five feet tall, with Fukushima seeing waves over thirty feet tall. Existing sea walls were not high enough, and many evacuation shelters

---

[8] Deutsche Welle article "Quake shifted Japan by over 2 meters," March 14, 2011.

were not located on high enough ground and were overrun with water when the ocean reached six miles inland. The unimaginable destruction took the lives of more than 18,000 people[9]. Had it not been for the early tsunami warnings, the death toll would have been much higher.

Whole towns and cities were flattened and washed away. Hundreds of thousands of vehicles were destroyed. The debris carried by the tsunami waters crushed everything in its path including over 45,000 buildings. Power lines were damaged causing 4.4 million people to lose electricity for weeks. The airport in the city of Sendai was flooded, and even Tokyo's major airports had to divert and cancel many flights. Trains stopped running all over the nation, effectively stranding millions of people.

Tokyo Disneyland closed for over a month after the earthquake. At least 20,000 guests at the park and many of the Cast Members working on the day of the earthquake could not go home since the mass transit systems stopped running, so they had to spend the night inside Disneyland in makeshift areas. My friends who work at Tokyo Disneyland told me stories of getting blankets and food to the thousands of stranded guests.

But all this was nothing compared to what happened at the Fukushima Daiichi Nuclear Power Plant just 140 miles north of Tokyo. All nuclear plants in the earthquake zone, including the Daiichi plant, started shutting down per safety procedures. And although they lost main power due to the earthquake, they were equipped with backup generators to power the water pumps that cooled the reactor cores. Reactors take time to cool down even after a shutdown, requiring a constant flow of water to be maintained. This water becomes radioactive and is therefore kept within a reactor containment vessel. The

---

[9] National Police Agency Report "Police Countermeasures and Damage Situation associated with 2011 Tohoku district - off the Pacific Ocean Earthquake," September 10, 2020.

contaminated water itself has to be cooled, which is done by a separate source of water that never touches radioactive material, so therefore does not become radioactive. All of this was working fine until the tsunami waves hit an hour after the earthquake and inundated the backup generators, which were located behind sea walls that were designed for "normal" tsunami waves. When the backup generators died, the staff at the nuclear plant quickly realized that a nightmare scenario was about to unfold, and they worked tirelessly, around the clock, to avert an even bigger nuclear disaster.

Without power, the pumps did not run. Without pumps, the water did not flow. And without water, the reactor fuel rods got too hot and melted down through the steel containment vessel. Over the course of several days, three of the six reactors melted down inside the reactor cores. The steel and concrete containment vessels around the reactors are designed to keep all radioactive materials inside as long as it is cooled properly. Without the proper cooling, steam pressure builds up inside and could explode the containment vessel causing a catastrophic release of radiation. That is what happened at Chernobyl in Russia, but *not* what happened in Fukushima.

At Fukushima, steam was able to be vented to prevent such a disaster. However, this still meant that some radioactive steam was released into the atmosphere. Hydrogen gas was also produced as a byproduct and quickly accumulated inside the building. It was this hydrogen gas that exploded *outside* the containment vessel, and which then spread the radioactive materials even further. The cores, although partially melted, were eventually stabilized.

A second, and possibly much bigger problem, was a separate holding tank of spent nuclear fuel rods that were being stored in the reactor buildings but not inside the containment vessel. They were stored in a simple water tank since they were not actively undergoing a reaction. However, when this water system also failed, it presented a second and greater danger since there was no containment vessel surrounding it. Some scientists have said that if this material had been released, a much larger area including all of Tokyo could have been affected.

It took the courage and dedication of the workers to get the situation controlled as much as possible. Firetrucks and hoses were brought in to spray fresh water into the exploded buildings so that the fuel rods were sufficiently cooled. At one point during the crisis, water-dropping helicopters were used to cool down these rods, as there was too much radiation to safely enter the buildings. Sea water was also pumped in at one point to help cool the reactors.

To this day, the molten fuel rods are still inside those reactors. It is still too dangerous for people to enter the buildings, so remote controlled robots have been used to help with the repairs and cleanup efforts. One of the biggest problems now is ground water and rainwater getting into the reactor buildings, becoming radioactive, and then seeping out into the sea. This radioactive water has been collected through the years and filtered and then stored inside massive tanks containing 1,000 tons of water each. Since this water is still radioactive, the solution thus far has been to keep building more and more tanks as they get filled. In the ten years since the accident, more than a thousand tanks have been built to collect over 1.2 million tons of radioactive water. In 2016, in an effort to slow this process, the ground around the power plant was frozen to make a wall of ice to slow the flow of seepage into the reactors. This seems to have slowed the water flow, but not entirely stopped it.

Although a much greater disaster was averted, the hydrogen gas explosions did spread enough radiation to force the evacuation of some 154,000 people from a nineteen-mile radius. Depending on the direction of the wind, the radioactive particles hit some towns much harder than others, although they were farther away. Many of the evacuation orders still stand to this day. The radioactivity that was released will not go away for decades if not longer, and sadly continues the ordeal for thousands of people.

As something you only read about or see on the news, the magnitude of such a disaster is difficult to comprehend. The hell that this area went through is scary to think about, but it should not be forgotten. As evacuation orders are lifted a little at a time, the Fukushima areas affected have very slowly started to return to life. There is even a trial program run by a local company to give tours of the area, with the goal of raising awareness and to promote the local businesses that have re-opened. Mass tourism is still not common, but I was able to secure a small tour of the Fukushima nuclear exclusion zone and the surrounding areas devastated by the earthquake and tsunami. It was a sad and sobering reminder of what happened ten years ago.

My visit started in Sendai, a city hit hard by the earthquake and tsunami. But given its distance from the nuclear plant, Sendai was not affected by the radiation and has, in many ways, recovered. From Sendai was an hour-and-a-half train ride south to Minami Soma City in Fukushima Prefecture. Minami Soma City was evacuated during the crisis and has now mostly returned. Being at the far north edge of the evacuation zone, they were lucky. At Haranomachi Station in Minami Soma City, I met my local guide, Taira Karin, along with four people from Europe. Karin-san drove us down to Namie, Futaba, and Okuma Towns approaching the heart of the nuclear exclusion zone. The nuclear exclusion zone is the area around the power plant hardest hit with radiation. Steel walls and chain link fences separated the area from the general public.

As our car slowly made its way past the checkpoint, we all looked at our personal radiation detectors. I knew that the radiation levels were going to be insignificant on the tour, but the somber mood made me a little paranoid. I had seen photos and news reports of the destruction on television, but this was all real, right in front of us.

I saw a wide-open field with only one building standing. It was damaged and crumbling, but it stood, whereas its neighbors were wiped away. Inside that building, near its front entrance, was a rack full of shoes. I saw a collection of high heels and slippers. I wondered how many had lived there, and if they survived. At a nearby field, I saw a pile of gravestones that must have weighed hundreds of pounds each, but which were still tossed about by the tsunami. With the tombstones swept away, many families lost the graves of their ancestors.

In the distance were piles upon piles of gigantic sandbags, each about a meter in diameter and height, stacked neatly as far as the eye could see. Karin-san informed me that instead of sand, these bags contained the radioactive topsoil collected from this area. As the radioactive particles spread from the power plant, they eventually settled on the ground, making the topsoil the most toxic part of the environment. The good news (if there is any) is that the topsoil can be bagged and removed from the area to make it safe for returning people to live. The bad news is that the bags now need to be stored somewhere until the radiation decays to much lower levels. Caesium-137, one of the main byproducts of nuclear fission, has a half-life of thirty years, which means that the soil would still be half as radioactive in thirty years. There is an urgent need for long-term safe storage. At the time of my visit, a permanent storage location was being built nearby for the nine million bags of radioactive dirt collected to date. I wondered how gigantic that building would be.

We drove to a farm where we saw around a hundred cows grazing in a field. I was told that these cows were all exposed to high levels of radiation and could not be sold for human consumption. The farmer there, however, refused to slaughter and destroy the animals and is now taking care of them until their natural deaths. He himself just wants to spend his last days there taking care of his animals—a sad, powerful reminder of how life can change in an instant.

In the midst of this tour of destruction, we approached what looked like a brand-new apartment complex. A sign in front of this multi-building complex identified it as housing for the local employees of TEPCO, Tokyo Electric Power Company, the owner of the Daiichi Nuclear Power Plant and its cleanup operations. Approximately four thousand employees are still working at the power plant (ten years later) to clean up and secure the site. The project manager in me could not fathom how much all this was costing, but it was a good sign that the government remains committed to the cleanup effort.

It is understandable that a large portion of the Japanese public is now adamantly against nuclear power plants. In fact, Fukushima Prefecture has vowed to power the region with 100% renewable energy by 2040. It is already at 40% renewable, being powered by solar and wind farms located throughout the region.

Finally, we stopped at an overlook with a direct view of the Fukushima Daiichi Nuclear Power Plant less than a mile away. I could see the four reactor buildings that had exploded and the repairs that had been made. I could see the gigantic water storage tanks filling every free space in-between the buildings, and I could see the calm blue waters of the Pacific just a few more yards away. Everything looked so clean, orderly, and peaceful, but looking at the calm blue horizon gave me chills as I imagined what the tsunami may have looked like from this vantage point.

As we left the exclusion zone, a checkpoint guard measured the radiation levels of the vehicle tires as well as each of our shoes. Since the ground is the most radioactive surface, we did not want to be tracking a lot of dirt outside of the zone. After being cleared, we checked our personal dosage meters to confirm that we were within the safety range. Mine read four microsieverts or about the equivalent to half of a dental x-ray.

Sidenote on radiation:

We are constantly being bombarded by background radiation from outer space and other natural sources. A typical dosage from these sources is around 2,400 microsieverts per year or 0.27 per hour. Therefore, on my five-hour tour, I received 1.4 microsieverts from natural sources. In comparison, a dental x-ray is around ten microsieverts, so I got a pretty low dose from the tour. In fact, I got a much higher dose of radiation from my flight from LA to Tokyo. Since commercial flights fly high above the protective atmosphere, you get around three to five microsieverts per hour of flight. That means you are getting the equivalent of a dental x-ray for every two to three hours of flying. Still way below the safety limit of 100,000 microsieverts for an increased cancer risk. A million microsieverts would cause immediate radiation sickness, but usually not death, so no need to worry about background radiation, dental x-rays, or visits to Fukushima.

Being a tourist, I was, of course, busy taking photos and videos of the new and interesting sights along the way, but I constantly needed to remind myself that this was all real. Not a museum display or an amusement park. This was where it all happened. Most sobering was the fact that it all happened less than ten years ago. I personally know several people who lived through the earthquake, and I remember watching the horror unfold on the evening news. The tour was understandably subdued and filled with respectful silence, but as sad as it was, there were positive notes to be found in the efforts to rebuild, clean, and recover from the disaster.

On our way back, we stopped in Namie town for some snacks and drinks. We went to a place called Grandma's Kitchen. As I was sitting at a table outside, the owner of the restaurant came out to talk to us. She thanked us for visiting Namie Town, which had only recently opened back up. Business was obviously down, with less than ten percent of its citizens having returned. She asked me where I was from and why I came to visit. With Karin-san acting as an interpreter, I explained that I wanted to learn about and see what had happened here for myself. I am drawn to unique and interesting places, and this was one of the most unique places in the world. I also wanted to help the area in a small way, since I had heard that tourism was one of the ideas to help generate income for the area. That is why this trial program started, and I was lucky enough to find it. Between puffs of smoke from her cigarette, she seemed happy to hear what I said. She told me about how difficult the tragedy was (without getting into specifics) and said that everyone who chose to come back was trying their best to regain a sense of normalcy. I thought I heard her say *"shouganai"*—a Japanese phrase that can be translated, roughly, as "it is what it is"—which made me appreciate how people who faced such unbelievable hardships could stay positive and have the will to carry on. Carry on Fukushima!

Sidenote on the phrase Shouganai (しょうがない):
One of the most interesting Japanese words and phrases that cannot be easily translated is *shouganai*. Often times it is simply translated as "it is what it is" or "it can't be helped," but it goes much further than that. It is not a defeatist attitude of just giving up when something doesn't go your way. It is the realization that there are many things in this world that are completely out of one's control, and that you should accept them, make the best out of the situation, and move on.

It may sound negative at first, but I believe the term is a rather positive way of approaching life, especially when faced with unimaginable catastrophes. Instead of giving up when facing daunting odds against you, I believe the attitude of *shouganai* enables you to accept the setback as a burden that you must bear and strive on regardless. Realizing that often times it will not be easy to move on, but accepting the cards that you are dealt, allows you to play with calm, knowing that you are playing the best hand that you possibly can. No complaints, no finger pointing, no revenge, no lawsuits.

Between devastating natural disasters, nuclear catastrophes, and a history long on tragic events, Japan offers the locals and tourists many opportunities to learn about and reflect on the ways in which life can change in an instant, and how the human spirit perseveres through challenging times. Other uniquely powerful, moving memorials and museums to visit in Japan are:

- Iwate Tsunami Memorial

- Kobe Earthquake Memorial Park

- Hiroshima Atomic Dome and Peace Museum

- Nagasaki Peace Park

Earthquake and tsunami damage

An abandoned town, still not safe
for residents to return.

One of many abandoned cars. They all had flat tires.

A school building showing the
water level mark of the tsunami.

New sea walls are being built higher than before.

Contaminated cows living out their lives in peace.

View of the Fukushima Daiichi Nuclear Plant;
Reactors 1, 2 and 3 experienced meltdowns.

Entering the Exclusion Zone

Large bags of contaminated soil

Around nine million of these bags
have been filled so far.

Everyone's shoes are checked for radiation.

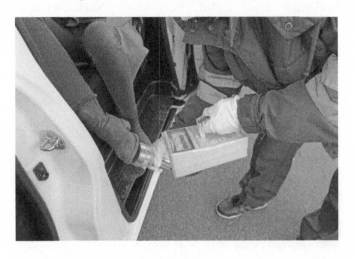

My total radiation dosage for the tour

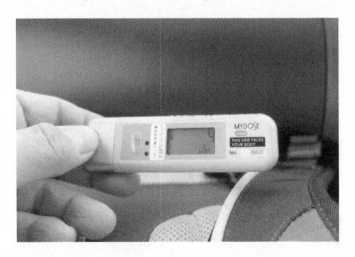

Karin-san has informed me that since the time of my visit, even more businesses have re-opened in Namie town. A road-side station, called Michi no Eki Namie, is now selling locally produced vegetables, saké, and pottery.

photo by Taira Karin

Some farmers have returned to Namie and Odaka towns and are providing locally grown vegetables for consumption. All vegetables are checked for radiation levels before being approved for sale.

photo by Taira Karin

The famous saké brand, Kotobukia (壽), is
produced locally by the Suzuki Saké Brewery.

photo by Taira Karin

An adjacent shop sells the local Soma Obori Pottery.

photo by Taira Karin

PART VI
NOURISHMENT FOR
THE BODY AND SOUL:
FOOD OF JAPAN / *WASHOKU* (和食)

I started this journey with food, and food will bring us full circle. When asked what it is about Japan that I love the most, it is most often the food that comes to mind. Specifically, the term *washoku*. Literally meaning "the food of Japan," the word generally stands for traditional Japanese cuisine and culture. *Washoku* cuisine is of such importance that UNESCO actually recognized it as an "Intangible Cultural Heritage of Humanity" in 2013 stating, "Washoku is a social practice based on a set of skills, knowledge, practice, and traditions related to the production, processing, preparation, and consumption of food. It is associated with an essential spirit of respect for nature that is closely related to the sustainable use of natural resources."

No matter where you are in Japan, a delicious meal is never that far away. If you don't know where to eat, all you have to do is to ask a local, "What is the famous food in this area?" There will almost always be an answer. Not only does every region, prefecture, and city have a specialty, but those specialties are often celebrated as a source of regional pride and identity.

There is no shortage of restaurants to try, either. Tokyo has approximately 150,000 eateries including 212 Michelin-starred restaurants, the most of any city in the world on both counts. (Paris, for example, has only half as many Michelin-starred restaurants as Tokyo.) Tokyo also has more than three times the number of restaurants as Paris, and more than five times Los Angeles and New York. With so much competition in such a densely packed space, it's no wonder that the quality of the food on offer is so high. From chain restaurants to hole-in-the-wall places, chances are good that a visitor to Japan will have an *oishii* meal. Just be open to try new things.

Often the restaurants in Japan are tiny places run by families, or even by one person. The smallest sit-down restaurant I've been to had six seats that barely fit inside the place, requiring the people near the door to get up to let others in and out. Many places have a ticket vending machine out front where you order your food. This allows the chef to focus on the cooking and rather than deal with menus, taking orders, or collecting money. Just choose what you want from the machine, pay up front, hand the printed ticket to the chef, and enjoy your meal!

The variety of food is diverse as well. Even within the umbrella of "Japanese food" there are a myriad of specialties and choices. But some common themes are shared across the board: Use the best ingredients, balance the flavors, and make it visually appealing. At the time of writing this book, I think I must have had around 1,300 meals in Japan. From simple snacks to eat on a train, to some of the most extravagant meals at Michelin-starred restaurants, I can safely say that I never went hungry in

Japan. Of those thousand-plus meals, many were quite memorable, either for the food, the service, or the atmosphere, and sometimes all of the above.

"So, what's for dinner?" It's a question often raised by me and my co-workers during breaks between long meeting sessions. We are, of course, in Japan to work, but something has to keep us going, and looking forward to a wonderful meal at the end of the day is always a comforting thought.

Osaka
大阪府

CHAPTER 17
JAPANESE FUSION: TAKEICHI (タケイチ)
Kitashinchi, Osaka

After wandering about the narrow and crowded streets of Osaka's Kitashinchi district, I spotted the small entryway with a white *noren* (doorway curtain) with the name Takeichi imprinted in English. There's a common saying that an old and worn *noren* is an indication of a popular and therefore good place. And Takeichi's *noren* was not new. A friend I was with actually thought that the curtain meant that the place was closed, when in actuality it means the exact opposite. We pushed past the *noren* and ascended a long and narrow staircase up to the restaurant above.

Known as the nation's kitchen, or *tenka no daidokoro*[10] (天下の台所), Osaka is home to good old "southern" cooking and "soul" foods like *okonomiyaki* and *takoyaki*[11], and offers traditional and nouveau cuisines alike. Spending most of my time near the Umeda

---

[10] The term originated in a non-food context, but it still applies here.

[11] Takoyaki is a snack made with wheat flour batter and octopus meat fried into a ball shape of about one inch in diameter, served with sauce.

area, I explored around to find unique and interesting places to eat. I only barely scratched the surface, since I probably walked past a hundred restaurants each night, having no clue as to what was being served inside most of them. This was particularly true in the Kitashinchi district, known for its multitude of hostess bars and high-end restaurants geared for business gatherings. This is where I had that first *kaiseki* meal, which introduced me to the world of Japanese food. And it's where I found Takeichi.

In a sea of a thousand restaurants, Takeichi stands out by offering a unique fusion of traditional Kyoto cuisine and western flavors. The chef-owner, Nakase Gakuya, prepares and cooks all the food himself, and comes around personally to each table to see how everyone is doing; not terribly difficult since the restaurant only has about three tables and a counter, but the personal touch is nevertheless appreciated, and it makes the dining experience enjoyable for all.

After graduating from the Tsuji Culinary Institute in Osaka, Nakase-san honed his craft at a restaurant and hotel in Kyoto. Fascinated by Italian, French, and other western cuisines, he aspired to create unique and original dishes that he had experimented with in school. He got his chance in 2011, when he opened Washoku Bal Takeichi in Osaka. Now in its ninth year, he is working every day to creatively combine traditional Kyoto cuisine with western techniques.

My first visit to Takeichi occurred during a business trip to Osaka when a couple colleagues from China and I were looking for something a little different. With a recommendation from another friend, we set out to find this small place near the Hilton Osaka. The place was small and crowded with businessmen and women. A few tables were along the north wall while an open-air kitchen completely occupied the south half. Nakase-san stood in the middle of the kitchen, surrounded by a short "L" shaped counter with less than ten seats. All around him were plates of food, an open-fire grill, burners, sink, and myriads of raw ingredients as well as a shelf full of spirits. He was obviously busy cooking several dishes all at once, when he saw us enter and greeted us with a healthy "*irrashaimase*!" or welcome!

We were met with smiles all around and seated. The small space was filled with a mixture of smoke from the grill as well as the smoking businessmen. The waitress didn't bother asking us if we wanted the smoking or non-smoking section as it was obviously all smoking. Despite this misfortune, I was still optimistic for a great meal. We were seated at the counter, getting a close-up view of the action. The appetizers were on full display along the counter, as the main dishes were being prepared on the grill. We received a menu printed in limited English, which helped, but Nakase-san also tried his best to explain some of the specials for the day. His English wasn't great, but good enough to get the message across. Soon we were presented with an interesting array of delicious dishes.

First was an appetizer made with eggs, pork, and vegetables baked (I think) into a solid form. It almost looked like a quiche except that it did not have a pastry crust. The texture was interesting, but the flavor was exquisite. A good start.

Next was a plate of tuna, yellowtail, and mackerel sashimi. Very nice! Fresh, not "fishy," with an optimal amount of dissolve-in-your-mouth fat and lean meat. A slight hint of freshly grated wasabi gave it the perfect kick. Next came Takeichi's trademark dish, piping hot tomato oden, an original creation by Nakase-san. Oden is a traditional Japanese dish where a variety of ingredients including vegetables, eggs, tofu, and fish are boiled in a soup-like concoction. The most popular ones are made with radishes and fishcake in a light soy flavored broth. Somewhat of a comfort food, many convenience stores and food carts will sell oden as a quick snack to warm you up during the winter. But this version was different. It was a whole tomato, peeled to expose the super-soft flesh inside, stuffed with ground pork, all in a light flavorful *dashi* soup. Served boiling hot in an individually-sized cast iron pot, each spoonful was a mixture of flavors from the sweet and tart tomato and the boiled meat inside—something I had never seen or tasted before. It was the highlight of the meal.

Soon the main courses came out to be shared by all. We got a seafood pasta dish, Japanese wagyu steak with grilled vegetables, and potatoes with avocado. Nakase-san prepared each dish superbly and gave us even more new flavors to dine on. The potatoes with avocado was another excellent dish, where the smooth texture of the avocado mixed nicely with the crispy skin of the fried potatoes. The western flavor was comforting after being in Japan for several weeks. And despite being fairly full by this point, I finished off the meal with a small bowl of *ochazuke* (tea over rice), like how an old lady from Kyoto would.

After the meal, as we were walking down the stairs and out the door, Nakase-san ran after us to say goodbye. I worried that some of the food would burn on the grill, but he seemed to have no concerns and was genuinely happy that we had visited him from faraway places. With such great food and atmosphere, I have returned to eat there several times, and have never left disappointed.

Owner and chef of Takeichi, Nakase Gakuya

Tomato oden, the signature dish of Takeichi

Wagyu steak with vegetables

Potatoes and avocado

Nara Prefecture
奈良県

CHAPTER 18
THE BEST HOT POT IN JAPAN:
KAWASEMI (かわせみ)
Nara City

Nara—famous for its temples and wild, free-roaming deer—is one of the few places in Japan *not* necessarily known for its food. So, finding a suitable restaurant for a nice business dinner was tricky whenever I had to go there, especially if we had a large group, as we normally did. But one night, while walking back to our hotels, my friend and colleague, Sasamori Shota, noticed a small unassuming restaurant called Kawasemi that advertised a unique dish called *kappa-nabe,* a hot pot of meat and vegetables stewed in a broth. This special place was so good, it turned into one of our treasured hangouts. Rich with delicious food as well as a charismatic chef who entertained us with stories throughout the entire dinner, the place is away from the usual tourist areas. They didn't even have an English sign out front, as I recall. The owner, Ohata Atsunori, ran it with his wife since opening the restaurant in 2006. I only ever saw the two of them, so it's likely they were the entire staff.

The first time we went, there were twelve of us—half Americans and half Japanese—and we essentially filled the entire restaurant. Luckily, the menu was simple, and we had ordered ahead of time. Honestly, I did not have any grand expectations of the place; I just hoped that it would be better than a generic *izakaya,* a type of Japanese bar-and-grill.

As soon as I entered, I felt a good vibe. First of all, not having an English sign out front was a good start, as it meant that they catered primarily to locals. The décor inside was simple and minimalistic, but modern and elegant. Subdued wood paneling lined the walls of the small space, with the tables matching the wood grain look. All the tables were pushed together to form one long arrangement to accommodate our large party. The tables had a couple of electric burners, which already had large clay pots on them. I did not see any other customers, so we would have the attention of the chef all to ourselves.

After a round of *kanpai* (cheers), we got our first taste of food: an appetizer of thinly sliced ham and pickles. It was tasty, but I was looking forward to the main dish, the hot pot of meat and vegetables. As the flavorful broth started to heat up in the pots in front of us, a mouthwatering aroma filled the air. Then came Ohata-san with a large platter stacked full of Japanese spinach called *komatsuna,* fried tofu, and a mound of carefully selected beef. The beef was extremely marbled, to the point of being mostly white, and sliced ever so thinly. Very similar to *shabu-shabu* (another hot pot dish), *nabe* features different vegetables and broth, and is simmered for a longer period. As Ohata-san started adding all the ingredients into the broth, I thought that it was going to overflow, but somehow, he got everything in and covered the pot with a lid. Just seeing the ingredients made my mouth water, but the aroma made my stomach growl with anticipation.

To my delight, Ohata-san was a talkative man, so it was good that joining us for dinner was a professional interpreter and friend of mine, Yuhara Toru. As Ohata-san prepared the *nabe*, he informed us that this was a version called *kappa-nabe*, in which beef is used instead of the usual fish and seafood. Originating in Nara, it was first invented as a way to cheaply feed the workers at meat packing plants. Ohata-san then took this concept and added in higher quality meats and developed a clearer, more refined *dashi,* or broth. This gave it a much lighter taste compared to typical *nabe,* which features a heavier and fishy taste. Ohata-san mentioned that he is pretty certain that no other place serves *nabe* quite like his, and he should know since he regularly attends a national competition of *nabe*, held annually in Kyoto Prefecture.

The event, called the Nabe One Grand Prix (鍋-1グランプリ), is held every December and features *nabe* restaurants from all over Japan. He proudly told us that the *nabe* that we were about to eat, had come in second place nationwide for the past three years. He also told us that it took him months of trial and error to develop the recipe of the *dashi*, and that finding the perfect cuts of beef was also challenging. Having worked in the meat industry, he knew how to spot the tasty cuts, so he opened this restaurant to serve his creations.

Wow, with that kind of introduction, I didn't know how a pot of beef, spinach, and tofu could possibly live up to that hype. I thought that this was all very interesting and entertaining, but wanted to judge the *nabe* for myself. I soon got my chance as Ohata-san scooped a ladle into small bowls for all to taste. *Itadakimasu.* We all took in a spoonful, and the reactions were immediate. *Oishii*! Yummy! OMG! This was incredible. The meat was so tender that it easily fell apart in my mouth. The spinach provided more texture and a satisfying "green" taste, while the spongy fried tofu soaked up the broth nicely to release the umami on to my taste buds. Not too heavy and with a slight salty taste, the broth was a perfect carrier of the beef and veggies. Using a bit of yuzu pepper, as recommended, gave it yet another dimension of flavor and a hint of citrus and spiciness. The combination of tastes and textures was so good that it felt like Ohata-san really had perfected all the minute details. That a bowl of *nabe* could be this memorable was completely unexpected. It shattered what I thought I knew about hot pots.

I returned there later that year during the winter, and everything was the same, except for the use of *mizuna* leaves and stalks (a type of mustard greens) instead of spinach. Eating a bowl of piping hot *nabe* was even more satisfying in the cold winter weather. Recently, Toru-san contacted the restaurant to help me with my research, and I learned that Ohata-san's *nabe* had finally won first place! I can't wait to return and have a celebratory pot of *nabe*.

Sasamori-san and Ohata-san

The summer ingredients: beef, spinach, tofu

The summer version

The winter version

Best *nabe* in Japan!

Hyogo Prefecture
兵庫県

CHAPTER 19
BETTER THAN KOBE BEEF:
SANDAYA HONTEN (三田屋本店)
Sanda, Hyogo Prefecture

Once again, I was in Japan on a business trip, and this time I found myself in Sanda, a small city about an hour north of Kobe. Sanda is home to several industries including manufacturing, chemical, pharmaceuticals, and foods. But it also is the home to Sanda beef, which gave me something to look forward to after work. Not as famous as Kobe beef, Sanda's own version of Japanese *kuroge* (black) beef is nonetheless regarded by many as being of higher quality than its Kobe cousin. With only a handful of farmers raising less than a thousand head of cattle each year, Sanda beef is even more rare than Kobe beef, and, in my opinion, better.

Sidenote on Kobe beef:
In the early 1900s, ranchers in Japan cross-bred local cows with newly acquired foreign breeds to produce what are known as wagyu (meaning Japanese cow). Four separate breeds were recognized as desirable, with the Japanese *kuroge* (black) being the most popular today.

Each breed is further divided into strains, with the Tajima strain being the most prized. Kobe beef comes from the Tajima strain of the Japanese black breed of wagyu cattle. To be branded as Kobe beef, the cattle must meet further requirements including:

- Must be born and raised in Hyōgo Prefecture.
- Processed at slaughterhouses in Kobe, Nishinomiya, Sanda, Kakogawa, or Himeji in Hyōgo Prefecture.
- Have a grade of A4 or higher and a marbling ratio of six or above.
- The weight of beef produced from each cow must be less than 1,036 pounds or 470 kg.
- Can be tracked via a serial number through every step of their life cycle.

The meat is valued for its flavor, tenderness, and fatty texture. The melting point of fat in Kobe beef is lower than that of common beef fat, which adds to the smooth texture. Only about 3,000 head of Kobe beef cattle are produced per year, making them a scarce and expensive commodity known the world over.

Not knowing a good Sanda beef restaurant, my colleagues and I asked a taxi driver for his recommendation. We figured in a small city like this, taxi drivers would probably be the most knowledgeable about such matters, and we were right. Immediately, the driver recommended a place called Sandaya. There were a few branches, but he specifically recommended their main branch, Sandaya Honten. We made a reservation and went for dinner on the following night.

As we arrived at the restaurant, I noticed that there were two Rolls Royces parked out in front. I wasn't sure if that was a good sign (of the restaurant's high quality) or a bad one (of its high cost and pretentiousness). Only one way to find out, I thought. We nervously entered and sat down in a spacious waiting area. We were soon greeted and shown into the main dining room. The place was huge. With more than two hundred seats, it was the largest restaurant I'd seen in Japan. The far wall of the building immediately caught my attention, as it was composed entirely of glass, two hundred feet wide. And behind the glass was an outdoor stage, surrounded by a Japanese garden and pond. The traditional architecture of the stage gave it away as a venue for Noh theater performances. They were not holding any performances that night, but even that empty backdrop was a stunningly beautiful setting for our meal. With a live pianist playing a concert grand in the background, I soaked in the ambiance and eagerly waited to start the meal.

Considering the atmosphere, prices weren't too high. I ordered the popular set course featuring a small-sized steak. Every entrée came with an all-you-can-eat ham appetizer, which, along with the steaks, was this restaurant's signature dish. We were told that the ham was locally made by aging, pickling, and then smoking the pork with cherry wood and coffee beans to give it a unique flavor. The ham was sliced paper thin and served with slivers of onion with a generous portion of a special dressing. The waiter did not describe the dressing, but I thought that I detected a hint of ginger. However it was made, it was all very delicious. I'm not a big fan of ham, but the appetizer did its job to prepare us for the main event.

The main course announced itself by sound and scent, even before being placed in front of me on the table. The unmistakable smell of grilled beef, with the sizzling sounds of a hot grill, surrounded our table as the servers brought out our meals. Each serving had a wooden platform with a cast iron plate on top. The iron was obviously hot as the meat and vegetables on it were being cooked as they were being served. The waiter explained that the steaks were raw, and that we were to cook them on the iron to our liking. Served on a bed of onions, the pre-sliced beef looked juicy and tender, even when raw. With my mouth already watering, I placed the beef on the iron plate to cook. As the butter that came on the steaks melted, the aroma became even more irresistible, and I couldn't wait any longer, so placed one of the pieces of meat in my mouth. There was an explosion of juiciness and flavor as the meat became like butter on my tongue. How could beef be so tender? As advertised, it tasted better than Kobe beef. (I personally think that Kobe beef is too fatty and has too strong of a taste.) This morsel was subtle, sublime, and just heavenly. Using the recommended *ponzu* sauce added a hint of citrus and salty taste to the flavor of beef. Each bite of Sanda beef was as delightful as the first. I finished off with a fruit sherbet for dessert. A fantastic meal all around.

I learned later that the founder, Koji Hirooka, had said, "The restaurant must satisfy all five senses of our customers, not just the taste. The main store is not just a restaurant, but a place for cultural arts. Meals need not only satisfy the appetite, but also satisfy the mind. We want to provide a dining space where you can feel the breath of art and culture." Sandaya Honten was created with that in mind. It is a place where both the appetite for food and culture can be marvelously satisfied.

Sandaya Honten - main dining hall

The Noh Theater Stage

The Ham Appetizer

The main course

A cut of the Tajima strain of the black wagyu beef

The high marbling ratio makes the beef very tender.

Tokyo
東京都

CHAPTER 20
A 200-YEAR-OLD RECIPE: NODAIWA
(野田岩)
Azabu, Tokyo

If you have a recipe that is two hundred years old and you've been selling that dish continuously, then you are probably on to something. Such is the case with Nodaiwa, a restaurant that has been serving *unagi* (freshwater eel) to *daimyo* (feudal lords) and commoners alike for the past five generations. Located just a few blocks away from Tokyo Tower, this Michelin-starred restaurant serves only the finest *unagi*, mainly from Shizuoka and Kagoshima Prefectures. They focus on fresh eels from the wild, although farmed ones are used as well, depending on the season. The main branch, in Azabu, is housed in an old folk-style building reminiscent of hundred-year-old-homes out in the countryside. In fact, the building is originally from a traditional village in Hida Takayama in Gifu Prefecture. It was dismantled, transported, and then reassembled in its current location.

The interior is elegantly decorated with traditional touches of wood and lacquer. My friends and I were lucky to get a reservation for a private room. We were led up a polished wooden staircase to the upper level. The second floor consisted of a long hallway with one side made entirely of traditional paper (*shoji*) screen doors. Separated by large wooden columns, each set of doors led to a private room. There was a running board of sorts elevated about six inches above the floor along the entire length of the hall, with another six-inch step up to enter each room. As is often found in Japan, this indicates a demarcation line of shoes vs. no shoes. We were to remove our shoes before stepping up on the running board and into the room. The room was small, with barely enough room for two tables and our party of six. The chairs were tiny as well, with arm rests only on the left side. I guess that made it easier to slide off the chair and exit? In any case, it was small even for my build, and way too small for some of my colleagues. After some shuffling around, we made it in and got ourselves situated for the meal to come.

The menu was simple. With a recipe going back two hundred years, there wasn't going to be many variations to the tried and true option, so I ordered a set course meal with their specialties, *shirayaki* and *unadon / unaju*. The *shirayaki* came first. The eel fillets were skewered and steamed slowly to remove excess fat and to soften the meat. They were then grilled over charcoal with very little sauce. Lesser unagi places often drench the meat with a thick teriyaki-like sauce, but Nodaiwa does not want to hide any of the fine flavors of the *unagi* itself and serves the *shirayaki* with almost no noticeable sauce. Delicate to the touch, it broke apart as soon as I grabbed it with chopsticks before it dissolved into a smooth mouthful. With the char marks from the flames visible, the eel had a very light flavor with a hint of smokiness. Along with some pickled vegetables, this served as a good appetizer for the main course to come.

Unadon is short for *unagi donburi*, which literally means eel bowl. You may recognize the "*don*" suffix from *katsudon, tendon, gyudon*, etc., which is just a bowl of rice with the main course on top, dribbled with sauce. Well, *unadon* was the very first manifestation of the *donburi* dish and was created around the time when Nodaiwa was founded two hundred years ago. Typically a fast food type of dish, *donburi* is found at places like Yoshinoya and convenience stores. But at a Michelin-starred place like Nodaiwa, you can bet that it will be on another level. One of the guys in our group got an *unadon*, but the rest of us got a fancier version, *unaju*, which is grilled eel on top of rice, served in a lacquered wooden box. Basically the same as an *unadon*, the *unaju* was larger in size and looked prettier. As the beautifully lacquered boxes were served, I could detect a slight aroma of grilled *unagi* as well as steamed rice. I removed the wooden lid and saw a flawless fillet of *unagi*, glistening with a light brown sauce, on top of a generous layer of white rice. My mouth watered in anticipation as I reached for my chopsticks.

The *unagi* was just as fluffy and light as the *shirayaki*, but it was basted with a larger amount of sauce made from *mirin* (rice wine) and soy sauce, to create a perfect balance of sweetness and saltiness. The rice below was warm enough to keep the *unagi* heated, but not too hot to over steam it. The bed of rice also soaked up the little bit of sauce dripping from the unagi, to provide that flavor in every yummy bite.

Although I was just a few blocks away from my high-rise hotel in Tokyo, sitting in that traditionally decorated building and eating a dish that originated two hundred years ago, I could thoroughly enjoy every last bite and imagine a *daimyo* doing the same during the Edo Period. Preserving such rich tradition and culture is a hallmark of *washoku* and should be sought out whenever possible. For this, Nodaiwa is a cultural gem.

Nodaiwa – Azabu, Tokyo

Shirayaki

Unaju set meal

The upstairs corridor

CHAPTER 21
MICHELIN-STARRED RAMEN:
JAPANESE SOBA NOODLES TSUTA (蔦)
Sugamo, Tokyo

When I heard of a ramen shop that had won a Michelin star, I knew I had to go try it out. At $20 a bowl, it was expensive for ramen, but it's still probably the cheapest Michelin-starred meal that you will find. In January 2019, I went to the main Japanese Soba Noodles Tsuta shop in Sugamo.

The place, with only eight seats, was tiny and wait times were typically several hours. Therefore, Tsuta instituted a ticketing system where you had to go early in the morning to get a time slot to come back for a meal. I went at 8 a.m., paid $10 for a reserved time slot of 11 a.m., and returned three hours later for my meal. After arriving at 11 a.m., I still had to wait in line outside the building, as they were running a bit behind schedule. Finally, after forty-five more minutes, I was able to enter the tiny restaurant.

Once inside, I purchased my choice of ramen at a ticket vending machine. I chose their specialty: *shoyu* (soy sauce) ramen with chicken dumplings and a boiled egg. As I sat down at the counter, I noticed a display case with all their awards, including the Michelin man, which, now that I was thinking about it, seemed absurd. How could a tire company be the leading authority on culinary excellence?

Sidenote on the Michelin Guide:

The tire manufacturer, Michelin, first published a road guide of France in 1900 to promote an increase in demand for the newly invented cars and their tires. The guidebook included information such as maps, listings of tire repair shops, hotels, and restaurants throughout France. The guidebook grew in popularity over the years as automobiles became commonplace. The restaurant section of the guide was especially popular, so Michelin increased its team of anonymous reviewers to scour the land for that perfect meal. Getting a positive review with "stars" awarded in the Michelin guide, quickly became a badge of honor.

Publication stopped during World War II, but in 1944 the American and British troops asked for the latest guide to be reprinted for military use. Apparently, Michelin's maps of France were the best and most up-to-date available. The guidebook started printing again shortly after the war and continues to lead readers to exquisite meals everywhere.

On the counter of this ramen shop was a sign that listed all the ingredients of the special bowl of noodles I had just ordered. The stone-milled noodles (made onsite every morning) were actually soba noodles made from premium flour from Hokkaido and Tochigi, salt from Okinawa, and natural soda ash from Inner Mongolia. The soup stock was made from special breeds of chickens: Syamorock from Aomori, Amakusadaio from Kumamoto, Kuroiwatsuchidori from Miyazaki, and Nagoya Cochin from Aichi. The fresh soy sauce was from

Wakayama, Koikuchi Soy Sauce from Nagano, and Usukuchi Soy Sauce from Hyogo. Additional ingredients included mussels, beef, porcini mushrooms, dried fish, and vegetables. And, to top it all off, was a layer of black truffle oil from Italy and balsamic truffle cream. Wow! I had no idea what such exotic ingredients would taste like, especially in a ramen, but I prepared myself to be amazed. At the bottom of the sign were big bold letters saying: "Please don't use cell phone while eating ramen. Please focus on ramen." They took their ramen seriously.

Soon my bowl arrived and with it, a bouquet of wonderful aromas. It didn't look any different than the $3 *shoyu* ramen at the company cafeteria, but my hopes were still high. I sipped some of the soup. It was clear and light with some subdued flavors I had a hard time identifying. Not too salty, not too strong, not at all fishy, and not too oily. It was much lighter and subtler than my usual go-to *tonkotsu*-style ramen, which is made of pork broth. Next, I tried the noodles. Firm and chewy, while holding the flavor of the soup, the noodles were, simply put, exquisite. As I slurped up the soba, the top layer of truffle oil thinly coated the noodles to give it a smooth, slippery feel as well as a kick of flavor. Finally, I tried their famous dumplings. The dumplings were like wontons (like a bowl of wonton min in Hawaii) but the skin was made with extra-long strips, such that even after eating the meat portion, there was still a long strip of dough that you had to slurp in like a noodle. Very tender and flavorful, the dumplings were a nice change of pace from the noodles.

As I continued to enjoy the meal, the Ramen Effect soon reared its ugly head. The Ramen Effect (as discovered by me and my friends) is when you are eating a bowl of noodles, and it seems like there are plenty of noodles left when, suddenly, you reach in with your chopsticks to find that all the noodles are gone! It is a step function of consumption, giving you very little warning as to when the meal is going to end. Just like that, my meal was done. I sat back and took in a deep breath to appreciate what I had just eaten. I muttered, *"Gochiso sama deshita,"* which literally means "it was a feast," but is something you say at the end of a meal to convey thanks for the food. With that and a quick nod to the chef, I walked back out into the cold winter air. Since then, I found out that the Sugamo branch has moved locations to Yoyogi-Uehara and they got rid of the reservation system. So now I guess you have to go early and just wait in line for your bowl of mouthwatering goodness.

Bonus fact:
Tsuta has an instant version sold at 7-11 convenience stores. A way to take a small version of the meal home with you, it was a surprisingly good bowl of instant noodles.

The Sugamo Branch

Trophies and awards

The Michelin starred bowl of noodles

Instant ramen at a nearby 7-11 store

CHAPTER 22
MY FAVORITE SUSHI:
FUKUZUSHI (福鮨)
Roppongi, Tokyo

Of all the food in the world, my absolute favorite is *Edomae nigiri sushi,* Edo-style sushi. A simple idea that started as a way to preserve fish with fermented rice, the practice has evolved into an artform to create some of the most succulent morsels in culinary arts. And the epicenter is, of course, Edo itself, better known as Tokyo.

Many of the best sushi restaurants are clustered in the Ginza district, but there are a few notable exceptions that offer extraordinary quality cuisine while maintaining a friendly and unpretentious atmosphere. At the top of my list is Fukuzushi in Roppongi, which I fortunately discovered a few years ago. I had been to many fancy sushi places in Ginza before, but those always needed reservations weeks in advance, were exorbitantly expensive, and had somewhat uptight atmospheres. So without a reservation on a Tuesday night, and with no expectations, my friend and I decided to try Fukuzushi which was within walking distance of our hotel. Located in the glitzy Roppongi district of Tokyo, where many places market exclusively to foreigners and tourists, Fukuzushi is a traditional and genuine, family run restaurant offering some of the best sushi in the world. It is owned and operated by the husband-and-wife pair, Toyohito and Masami Agarie, who are the fourth-generation owners of Fukuzushi, which first opened in 1917.

Although in Roppongi, the restaurant is in a back alley of sorts, away from the crowds and the main roads. Walking toward it, my friend and I found ourselves in a dark, deserted alley with no one else in sight. We thought we were lost until we saw the entrance, which had a small Japanese style rock garden and a sign. As we walked into the building the dark mood quickly changed as Masami-san greeted us with a big smile and welcomed me and my friend to Fukuzushi. Both Masami-san and Toyo-san spoke English very well and made us feel instantly welcome.

The place was big compared to most sushi restaurants, with a counter that had more than twelve seats, several more tables in the main dining room, and a bar lounge area. The décor was modern with several traditional Japanese touches, but, honestly, what I noticed the most was the large display of fresh seafood in front of me as I sat down at the counter. I was a bit hungry so went with the *omakase* (chef's choice) course of fourteen *sushi* pieces, including a giant *temaki,* or hand roll. I love trying out new sushi places in Japan, so my excitement grew as Toyo-san prepared the opening course.

I saw him reach for a large slab of red tuna and slice off a perfect amount to top a nugget of rice. Was he going to start us off with *akami* (lean tuna)? Most sushi places I've been to start the meal with a less flavorful white fish or squid, but Toyo-san was jumping right into my favorite, tuna. And not just *akami*. Next came *chutoro* (medium fatty tuna), *aburitoro* (seared tuna), and *ootoro* (fatty tuna). The *akami* was smooth as silk and the soy sauce marinade tickled my taste buds as I bit into the lean slab of meat. The vinegar flavored rice made me salivate as soon as it landed on my tongue, and mixed perfectly with the fish on top, finishing off with a hint of freshly grated wasabi. To me, the quality and taste of the rice is just as important as the fish, and Fukuzushi got it right every time.

The *chutoro* and *ootoro* were even smoother. The fatty meat just dissolved into a burst of flavor. How could raw fish melt in your mouth? I didn't question it too much, and just kept eating. The *aburitoro* offered a new taste with its seared, smoky flavor, which was a nice change of pace. I finished off each bite with sips of hot green tea, my beverage of choice for a sushi meal, and with slices of *gari* (pickled ginger) to cleanse the palate. Soon enough, I was ready for the next round.

Next came *shimaaji* (amber jack), *hotategai* (scallop), and *ebi* (shrimp). All served raw, the scallop was shucked right in front of us for the freshest, sweetest taste possible. The shrimp was also fresh. (I thought I saw them move just before being served.) I don't think I had ever eaten raw scallops or shrimp before, but to my surprise they were pretty tasty. Glistening with a thin coating of soy sauce, each piece was firmer in texture than the tuna, but still broke apart easily as I chewed to release all the flavors.

Next up were the two *gunkanmaki* or "battleship rolls" which are the vertically rolled pieces of *nori* (seaweed) with rice on the bottom and fish on top. The first one had *ikura* (salmon eggs), while the second had *uni* (sea urchin). I feel like of all the typical sushi ingredients, these two are often done poorly at lesser restaurants. If *ikura* and *uni* are of poor quality, then they can be really bad, with a strong fishy smell and taste.

Thankfully that was not the case here, with the *ikura* eggs literally bursting with flavor as I chewed, while the smooth texture of the *uni* was spectacular. I think good *uni* tastes like cream—just divine.

Following the *uni* was *aji* (horse mackerel) with chopped *negi* (spring onions) and grated ginger. And then *anago* (sea eel), which was the only cooked selection of the night. Typically served with a sauce made of soy sauce, mirin, and sugar, the warm *anago* broke apart in my mouth in a mash of sweet umami. After more than ten pieces of nigiri, I was getting a little full, but gladly made room for the next round, which was the largest serving of the meal. It was a giant handroll or *temaki*, made of two separate pieces of *nori* and required both hands to hold properly. They called it the "negitoro temaki burger" and it was made with minced tuna and spring onions with a generous helping of rice rolled up into a tube of seaweed. I accepted the challenge with both hands and bit in. As I said earlier, the quality of the rice is very important for sushi, and this handroll did not disappoint. Even though I was getting full, I finished the *temaki* in no time.

As the end of the meal approached, there were only two more pieces left to go. Most *omakase* meals end with a serving of *tamago* (egg usually flavored with shrimp), and this meal was no different. However, before the *tamago*, Toyo-san made a surprising move. He asked me what I would like for my last piece. That was the first time that had ever happened to me during an *omakase* meal, so I had to collect my thoughts and try to come up with something that wasn't already served. It didn't take long for me to say, "*nodoguro kudasai.*"

Nodoguro, literally meaning black throat, is a seabass or seaperch that has a distinctive black color on the inside of their throats. A white fish caught from the Sea of Japan, it gained notoriety when after the 2014 U.S. Open, the tennis player and finalist, Nishikori Kei, said in an interview that he wanted to eat *nodoguro* when he got back home. Having come from Shimane Prefecture on the Sea of Japan coast, Nishikori must have missed *nodoguro,* which was not a well-known delicacy outside his home region. Now it is ubiquitous at sushi restaurants all over Japan and is one of my favorites. Fatty and tender, the *nodoguro* was served slightly seared like the *aburitoro*, and was a luxurious ending to this masterpiece of a meal.

Keeping the *washoku* tradition alive now for four generations, Fukuzushi is a gem worth seeking out. The top-notch sushi and friendly and accessible atmosphere made Fukuzushi one of my favorite restaurants and a place to return to on every visit to Tokyo. I can't wait to go again.

Entrance to Fukuzushi

The friendly chefs

Omakase dinner

Head Chef, Agarie Toyohito

For more exceptional meals, be sure to reserve a table at these restaurants:

- Kaizu Honten (Matsusaka Beef) in Matsusaka, Mie

- Atsuta Horaiken (hitsumabushi) in Nagoya

- Anywhere on Utsunomiya's Gyoza Street, Tochigi

- Sushi Kanesaka in Ginza, Tokyo

- Tempura Kondo in Ginza, Tokyo

- Shabuzen (shabu shabu) in Roppongi and other locations

- Any Sanuki Udon place in Kagawa

- Ichiran Ramen in Fukuoka and many more locations

POSTSCRIPT

Well, I hope you enjoyed that journey as much as I did. Writing about these experiences really took me back to those days of wonder and fascination. Hopefully, I can get back to Japan soon (after COVID-19) and start on a new journey of discoveries and adventures. As you may have gleaned, Japanese culture is an intricately complex world that is always changing, always evolving, but still staying true to its past and traditions. Although I barely scratched the surface, I hope I was able to give you a glimpse of that world and perhaps ignite a curiosity that will prompt you to make discoveries of your own. *Matane!* (またね) See you again!

Visitor Information

1. Seki Traditional Swordsmith Museum
   9-1 Minamikasugacho, Seki City, Gifu Pref.
   Tel: +81-0575-23-3825
   https://sekikanko.jp/

2. Nikko Woodcarving Center, Tochigi Prefecture
   2848 Tokorono , Nikko-shi, Tochigi 321-1421
   Tel: +81-0288-53-0070
   https://www.n-kibori.jp/
   https://www.youtube.com/watch?v=bytwCruJmWg

3. Sanjo Great Kite Battle, Niigata Prefecture
   Sanjo-Tsubame Public Field, Sanjo
   https://www.city.sanjo.niigata.jp/en/explore/events/1
   215.html
   https://www.city.sanjo.niigata.jp/material/files/group
   /11/000059957.png (map)

4. Bull Fighting, Niigata Prefecture
   Koguriyama, Ojiya
   Ojiya City Tourism, tel: +81-0258-83-3512
   https://enjoyniigata.com/en/spot/42381

5. d:matcha (tea farm & store), Kyoto Prefecture
   Kyomachi-17, Kamatsuka, Wazuka, Sorakugun,
   Kyoto, Japan 619-1212
   Tel: +81-774-74-8205
   https://www.dmatcha.com/

6. Sengakuji Temple, Tokyo
   2-11-1 Takanawa, Minato-ku, Tokyo
   Tel: +81-03-3441-5560
   http://www.sengakuji.or.jp/about_sengakuji_en/

7a. Sumida Hokusai Museum, Tokyo
2-7-2 Kamezawa, Sumida-ku, Tokyo
https://hokusai-museum.jp/?lang=en

7b. Hokusai Museum, Nagano Prefecture
485 Obuse, Obuse-machi, Kamitakai-gun, Nagano
Tel: +81-026-247-5206
https://hokusai-kan.com/en/

7c. Ganshō-in Temple
604 Karida, Obuse, Kamitakai District, Nagano 381-
0211, Japan
Tel: +81-026-247-5504
www.gansho-in.or.jp

8. Miho Museum, Shiga Prefecture
300 Tashiro Momoya, Shigaraki-cho, Koka-shi
Tel: +81-0748-82-3411
http://www.miho.or.jp/en/

9. Garinko II Ice Breaker Boat, Hokkaido
Marine Park, Monbetsu City, Hokkaido
Tel: +81-0158-24-8000
https://o-tower.co.jp/
https://www.youtube.com/watch?v=pa8Ey6rBn2Q

10. Mushing Works Sled Dog Tours, Hokkaido
Urimaku Nishi 31-25 Katogun Shikaoi Hokkaido
https://h-takarajima.com/otour/index/592
https://www.youtube.com/watch?v=LWPn6PauOv0
&t=3s

11. Zero Paragliding School, Tottori Prefecture
    Tottori Hamasaka 1-chome 16-45-2
    Tel: +81-080-1939-6640
    http://www.zero-para.co.jp/

12. Shimanami Kaido, Hiroshima and Ehime Prefectures
    https://shimanami-cycle.or.jp/go-shimanami/
    https://www.youtube.com/watch?v=gPo8lslThBA
    https://vimeo.com/326080490 (link for Japan)

13. Mt. Fuji Subaru 5th Station, Yamanashi Prefecture
    http://www.fujiyama5.jp/index02.html

14. Kurobe Gorge, Toyama Prefecture
    Hotel Kurobe
    7 Unazukionsen, Kurobe 938-0282 Toyama
    Tel: +81-765-62-1331

15. The Metropolitan Area Outer Underground
    Discharge Channel, Saitama Prefecture
    720 Kamikanasaki, Kasukabe City, 344-0111
    https://www.ktr.mlit.go.jp/edogawa/gaikaku/

16. Daiichi Nuclear Power Plant, Fukushima Prefecture
    Real Fukushima Tours
    1-30 Nishikicho, Haramachi-ku Minamisoma City
    https://real-fukushima.com/

17. Takeichi, Osaka
    1-9-15 Sonezakishinchi, Kita-ku, Osaka
    Tel: +81-050-3628-7228
    https://bal-takeichi.business.site/

18. Kawasemi, Nara Prefecture
    2-2 Sanjomiyamaecho, Nara City
    Tel: +81-0742-35-2918
    http://kawasemi-nara.com/

19. Sandaya Honten, Hyogo Prefecture
    7-5 Mukogaoka, Sanda City 669-1544
    Tel: +81-0120-711-863
    https://sandaya-honten.co.jp/

20. Nodaiwa, Tokyo
    Tel: +81-03-3586-9058
    http://www.nodaiwa.co.jp/english.html

21. Japanese Soba Noodles Tsuta, Tokyo
    3-2-4 Nishihara, Shibuya-ku, Tokyo B1
    Tel: +81-03-6416-8666
    https://www.tsuta79.tokyo/

22. Fukuzushi, Tokyo
    5-7-8 Roppongi, Minato-ku, Tokyo 106-0032
    Tel: +81-03-3402-4116
    http://www.roppongifukuzushi.com/

Video highlights from the locations visited:
https://youtu.be/-DU2joe5qlo

Visit: https://CulturalKaiseki.com

ABOUT THE AUTHOR

Born in Korea and raised in the U.S., Phil Lee started traveling the world at an early age. Living in diverse places such as: New York, Alabama, Korea, California, Florida, and China, getting accustomed to new cultures and environments was nothing new when he started traveling to Japan on frequent business trips. Now, with more than fifty trips to Japan under his belt, his appreciation and love of Japanese culture grows with every visit. This is his first book about his journey through Japan.

photo by Andrew Lee

Made in the USA
Las Vegas, NV
03 April 2021

20757011R00142